# Lighthouses of New York State

A Photographic and Historic Digest

of New York's Maritime Treasures

## Rick Tuers

Terri Tuers, Editor

Foreword by James Hyland,
The Lighthouse Preservation Society

Schiffer Publishing Ltd®

4880 Lower Valley Road   Atglen, Pennsylvania  19310

**Other Schiffer Books on Related Subjects**
*Alaskan Maritime.* Jim Gibbs.
*Ghostly Beacons: Haunted Lighthouses of North America.* Therese
    Lanigan-Schmidt.
*Lighthouse Views.* Tina Skinner & Mary Martin Postcards.
*Lighthouses of Cape Cod & the Islands.* Arthur P. Richmond.
*Touring New Jersey's Lighthouses.* Mary Beth Temple & Patricia
    Wylupek.
*Twilight on the Lighthouses.* Jim Gibbs.

Designed by Mark David Bowyer
Type set in Bernhard Modern BT / Aldine721 BT

ISBN: 978-0-7643-2692-9
Printed in China

Published by Schiffer Publishing Ltd.
4880 Lower Valley Road
Atglen, PA 19310
Phone: (610) 593-1777; Fax: (610) 593-2002
E-mail: Info@schifferbooks.com

For the largest selection of fine reference books on this and
related subjects, please visit our web site at
**www.schifferbooks.com**
We are always looking for people to write books on new
and related subjects. If you have an idea for a book please
contact us at the above address.

This book may be purchased from the publisher.
Include $3.95 for shipping.
Please try your bookstore first.
You may write for a free catalog.

In Europe, Schiffer books are distributed by
Bushwood Books
6 Marksbury Ave.
Kew Gardens
Surrey TW9 4JF England
Phone: 44 (0) 20 8392-8585; Fax: 44 (0) 20 8392-9876
E-mail: info@bushwoodbooks.co.uk
Website: www.bushwoodbooks.co.uk
Free postage in the U.K., Europe; air mail at cost.

# Dedication

I would like to dedicate this book to Jesus, who is the Light of the World, and to all men and women who have helped light the way to safety for mariners throughout New York's history.

# Contents

# List of Figures

*"Ye are the light of the world. A city that is set on a hill cannot be hidden. Neither do men light a candle, and put it under a bushel, but on a candlestick; and it giveth light unto all in the house." Matthew 5:14-15*

# Foreword

Having lived in upstate New York for a number of years, and having married a native New Yorker, I have a special fondness for the lights of this great state, many of which I've visited while exploring the varied shorelines of the state's ocean, lakes, and rivers. While living in the area of Rochester, New York, I was delighted to discover that the state had a large number of inland lighthouses. It has been my observation that those who are unfamiliar with the state, and tend to think of lighthouses as buildings that are primarily found at the ocean, are often surprised at the revelation that there are scores of these fascinating structures spread out along the hundreds of miles of inland waterways that ring New York on three of its four sides – north, east, and west. Like exclamation marks along the shore, people are naturally drawn to them. Whether encountering them alone on solitary explorations, or on outings in the company of family and friends, I have always sought them out, finding them to be a great source of inspiration.

The telling of the story of New York's lighthouses has been a long-awaited event for many of us, who have a fascination for these remarkable buildings. Until now, the story has only been told piecemeal, at best. Because the state of New York is so large and diverse, having several distinct geographical areas, there has been a tendency to tackle this subject, if at all, on a regional basis.

There are a few books out there that include some limited information about New York's lighthouses, but until now, the record has been incomplete; so figuratively speaking, we have seen a few trees, but not the forest. In the past, for instance, we have seen mention made in some books of the Atlantic Ocean lighthouses surrounding Long Island, and in other publications, the lake lights of Ontario, Erie, and Champlain have been featured, but have generally been restricted to literature about the individual lakes. Then again, the various river lights, such as those found on the Hudson, St. Lawrence, and Niagara Rivers have received a bit of coverage, but mostly on a regional basis. In addition, there are the many "lost" lights of New York State – those that have been decommissioned and have fallen vacant, or sold off to private hands. Until now, no one has pulled all this information together and presented it to the public in publication form. It has remained fractured and incomplete. We have never before seen a complete picture of the whole subject matter of lighthouses in the great State of New York.

The reasons for this state of affairs have been numerous. First and foremost among the reasons is the poor state of lighthouse record keeping over the years. With the changing of federal bureaucracies responsible for the lights, the widespread dispersal of old paperwork to various federal record centers over the years, fires at the National Archives that have destroyed a significant number of documents, the widespread practice of pilfering important historical documents and memorabilia for keepsakes, together with the absence of a Coast Guard historian's office until recent years to bring order out of chaos, much has been lost.

Therefore, tackling this subject, and bringing together all the loose strings, has been a monumental feat. When I first met Rick Tuers at a lighthouse slide show lecture I delivered to the Schenectady Camera Club, he was looking for some direction in applying his considerable talents to tackling the subject of lighthouses. I encouraged him to focus on New York's lighthouses because, in terms of research, it was such a "black hole" for those of us who were trying to pull together the pieces of the story. With so many beacons out there, and so many "lost" lights that were no longer functional or had fallen into private hands, it was difficult for those of us in the lighthouse movement to comprehend the extent of what was out there and what kind of condition these New York lights were in. Clearly, someone needed to take on this massive research project, and Rick seemed to have the ability and resolve to take it on.

The fruits of Rick's considerable labors, spanning many years, are found in the pages that follow. I highly recommend them to you. This survey is a significant undertaking because, to my mind, it represents the largest single missing piece of the puzzle to understanding our nation's lighthouse heritage. I applaud Rick for his efforts to bring together this important historical material in a comprehensive way for the first time. It is a remarkable achievement in the documentation of America's lighthouse history.

—James Hyland, President/Founder
The Lighthouse Preservation Society

# Acknowledgments

During the last fifteen years that it has taken me to photograph, secure a contract, and write this book, many generous and talented individuals have given their time and shared their gifts to make this opportunity possible. Some individuals I have named here, while many will be nameless, since there are too many to mention. I have received boat rides to photograph many of the water bound lighthouses. Many have given me permission to enter the inner confines of the lighthouses and photograph areas that would otherwise be off limits.

The Coast Guard served as my "Guardian Angel" on more than one occasion as I rowed a 12-foot boat in the St. Lawrence River to photograph Cross Over Island lighthouse and paddled my kayak in 3-foot seas in Peconic Bay to shoot Long Beach Bar. They also helped me with many photo shoots to several offshore sites, capturing many images here in this book.

I would like to thank my wife, Terri, for her inspiration, encouragement and her meticulous and tireless dedication to editing. To my mom and dad, for giving me my first camera when I was seven years old. To my son Greg, for the many side trips on our vacations to "take one more picture." To James Hyland, of the National Lighthouse Preservation Society, for writing the Forward. To my map maker, Bruce Willett; Chris Persans, for her wonderful graphic illustrations; Ed Blackmer, for guiding me to the Crossover Island Lighthouse; Jim Crowley and Aram Terchunian, for their insight; Pat Ralston, for her dedication to preserving Hudson River lighthouses; Susan Schermerhorn, Jerry Spaziani, Charlie Grime, Chris Schubert and Chief Robert Milmo from the Coast Guard, for assisting with boat rides necessary for the water-based photography; Deb Lacascio, for assistance with research; Mike Oliviere, for proof reading; and the Hudson Athens Lighthouse Preservation Society. I would to especially thank Betsy White and Dick White, of the Montauk Historical Society, for their unconditional support of my photography and their encouragement to write a book, dedicated to New York lighthouses.

# One – Introduction

Before I moved to New York State, I never had traveled to see a lighthouse, except for the Statue of Liberty, on my third grade field trip. Every summer, like clockwork, our family would vacation at the New Jersey seashore, along a barrier island on Barnegat Bay. I have fond memories of spending every waking moment clamming in the bay, strolling along the beaches, or body surfing in the ocean. The lure of the ocean has become a ritual I still enjoy today with my work for the state of New York. Most of my vacations with my family are ocean centered.

After I moved to New York, I was amazed at the number of diverse ecosystems found here. New York is the only state in the country that contains all five classes of water bodies: rivers/streams, lakes/reservoirs, estuary waters, ocean coastline, and wetland acres. It has over 52,000 miles of streams and rivers; 800,000 acres of lakes/reservoirs; 1,500 square miles of estuary waters; 120 miles of ocean coastline; 577 miles of Great Lakes shoreline, 2.4 million acres of freshwater wetlands; and 25,000 acres of tidal wetlands. New York has the Erie and Champlain Canals, the scenic Hudson River, the majestic Lake Champlain, and the busy St. Lawrence Seaway.

Where there is water and navigation, there are beacons of hope -- lighthouses. And New York is no exception. There are 69 lighthouses in New York, more than Maine, which has only 65. From the tip of Easthampton on Montauk Point to the northwest corner on Lake Erie, where the majestic Buffalo Main Lighthouse stands, New York has an array of lights, all shapes, colors, and sizes, and many within driving distance of each other.

To the ordinary observer, a lighthouse is just a historic landmark, or a destination on a vacation. To the lighthouse aficionado, known as a pharologist, the beach and surf, the history, the romance, the heroism, and the engineering and architecture is a fascination that is shared in this book.

Chapter Two contains a brief history of America's lighthouses, including a list of lighthouses that were constructed prior to the signing of the Declaration of Independence. It also details the history of the Lighthouse Administration and how it evolved from the Lighthouse Establishment, to the Lighthouse Service, to the Lighthouse Board, and in 1939 to the U.S. Coast Guard. Chapter Three describes the lamps, Fresnel lens, and twelve engineering types of lighthouses. In addition, this chapter details some the construction challenges encountered in building the New York lights and provides a description of the fuels used prior to electricity.

**Map 1. New York Lighthouses**

The remaining chapters present a tour of the New York State Lighthouses, organized regionally and chronologically. The tour starts in Long Island (Chapter Four), and heads west and north from New York City (Chapter Five), to the Hudson River Valley (Chapter Six), Lake Champlain (Chapter Seven) and the Seaway Trail (Chapter Eight) – which includes Lake Erie, Niagara River, Lake Ontario, and the St. Lawrence River. In Chapters Four through Eight, the regional history, culture, and environmental setting are noted, along with the unique features of each light, the background of its establishment, and stories of shipwrecks and rescues. These chapters also include stories of some of the keepers and their families, and directions to each lighthouse.

Some lighthouses have fallen to disrepair and have been extinguished or demolished. Chapter Nine, the Lost Beacons of New York, contains a brief listing and description of the 15 beacons that were once part of New York's maritime history.

Each lighthouse is a distinct mile marker in history with a unique past, full of personal history of the keepers, families, and their lives. The lighthouse keepers and their assistants interacted with mariners and shippers who depended on them to keep the light shining brightly. Often, the keepers and their families were called to save lives. Some interesting accounts of keepers' lives are contained in Chapter Ten. There is also a bibliography and glossary for the vigilant pharologist.

Most people in twenty-first century America would find being a lighthouse keeper more than challenging. With most lighthouses in remote locations, keepers and their families lived solitary lives. Only by traveling to these lights and spending time there, does one get a sense of the situations they must have faced. The dedicated workers of the Lighthouse Board, known today as the U.S. Coast Guard, assisted mariners and cargo vessels transport goods to and through New York State to the Midwest and to Europe.

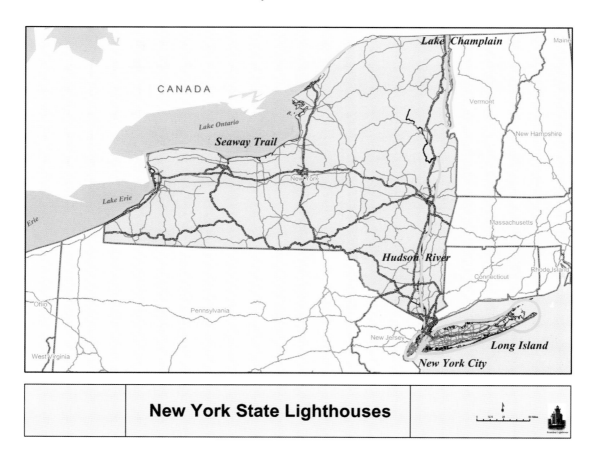

**New York State Lighthouses**

Over the past 30 years, the Coast Guard has divested itself of maintaining the structures and grounds of the lighthouses throughout the United States. All of the beacons in America, except for the Boston Lighthouse, are now automated. Devoted groups of volunteers have formed preservation societies to adopt, save, and maintain these pearls of American maritime history for future generations to enjoy. A list of some of the national groups is contained in Appendix Two, along with groups in New York State. Appendix Three is a list of the maritime museums in New York State. Many of these museums also sponsor tours to the beacons in their vicinity. Appendix Four contains the websites of the lighthouses and maritime museums in New York State. Since times of tours and events are always changing, it is suggested that the website be consulted for the most up-to-date information on events.

To the trained eye, each lighthouse has its own personality or characteristics, such as color, flashing frequency and duration, much like human DNA. Although some lighthouses may look like one another, there are no two exactly alike. The Coast Guard maintains a Light List which contains locations and characteristics for each light, by region of the United States.

I hope that after you read this book you will have a deeper appreciation of the role that lighthouses, keepers, and the Lighthouse Service and later the Coast Guard had in settling and helping our young nation to grow. I hope you will see each lighthouse as a unique history lesson with hundreds of personal stories that would fill volumes of libraries.

### The Light-Keeper

The brilliant kernel of the night,
The flaming light room circles me:
I sit within a blaze of light
Held high above the dusky sea.

Far of the surf doth break and roar
Along bleak miles of moonlight shore,
Where through the tides the tumbling wave
Falls in an avalanche of foam
And drives its churned waters home
Up many an undercliff and cave.

The clear bell chimes: the clockwise strain,
The turning lenses flash and pass,
Frame turning within glittering frame
With frosty gleam of moving glass:
Unseen by me, each dusky hour
The sea-waves welter up the tower
Or in the ebb subside again;
And ever and anon all night,
Drawn from afar by charm of light,
A sea bird beats against the pain.

And lastly when dawn ends the night
And belts the semi-orb of sea,
The tall, pale pharos in the light
Looks white and spectral as may be.
The ebb is out: the green
Straight belt of seaweed now is seen,
That round the basement of the tower
Marks out the interspace of tide;
And watching men are heavy-eyed,
And sleepless lips are dry and sour.

The night is over like a dream:
The sea-birds cry and dip themselves:
And in the early sunlight, steam
The newly bared and dripping shelves,
Around whose verge the glassy wave
With lisping wash is heard to lave;
While, on the white tower lifted high,
The circling lenses flash and pass
With yellow light in faded glass
And sickly shine against the sky.

— Robert Louis Stevenson

# Two – History of America's Lighthouses and the Administration

### First Lighthouses in America

The first lighthouses in North America were constructed to safely navigate between Boston, New York, and Philadelphia. After America was colonized, trade routes were established, and maps were made based on captains' log books. Shallow sand bars, reefs or rock outcrops were often found by accident. The lessons learned were capitalized on by placing markers and updating navigation maps.

It is believed that the tower erected in 1716, on Little Brewster Island in Boston Harbor, was the first North American lighthouse. This lighthouse was blown up during the Revolutionary War and later rebuilt in 1783. However there is some evidence that an earlier lighthouse was built in Havana, Cuba in 1671. Whichever light was the first in North America is not as important as to know that American Colonial lighthouses were built by states through taxes and lotteries.

The Boston Lighthouse was followed by Brandt Point, Massachusetts (1746); Beavertail, Rhode Island (1749); New London, Connecticut (1760); Sandy Hook, New Jersey (1764); Cape Henlopan, Delaware (1765); Charleston, South Carolina (1767); Plymouth, Massachusetts (1768); Portsmouth, New Hampshire (1771); Cape Ann, Massachusetts (1771); Great Point, Massachusetts (1784); and Newbury, Massachusetts (1788).

### Early Administration

President George Washington was a big promoter of lighthouses. In 1789, he urged Congress to recognize lighthouse construction as a national priority. Congress responded by passing its ninth piece of legislation on August 7, 1789, which created the Lighthouse Establishment, later becoming the Lighthouse Service. Congress assigned the aids to navigation to the Department of the Treasury under Alexander Hamilton. Presidents Washington, Adams, and Jefferson personally approved the construction contracts for lighthouses. They also appointed and dismissed lighthouse keepers. In 1792, Hamilton assigned this responsibility to the Commissioner of Revenue.

Figure 2-1. East Coastal Lighthouse

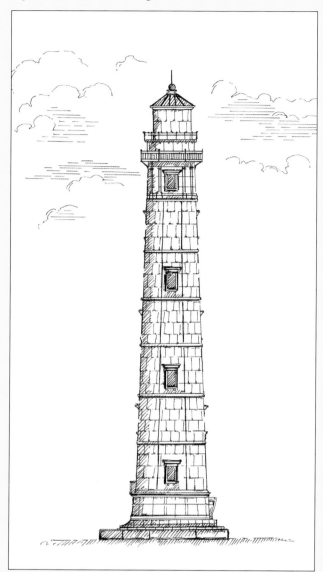

## Lighthouse Service's First Projects

When the Lighthouse Service was in its infancy, the number of lighthouses in operation was very small. To remedy this, a major construction program added a dozen lighthouses by the end of the eighteenth century. Lighthouses were completed or started at Cape Henry, Virginia (1791); Portland Head, Maine (1791); Tybee, Georgia (1791); Sequin, Maine (1795); Bald Island, North Carolina (1796); Montauk Point, New York (1797); Baker's Island, Massachusetts

(1798); Cape Cod, Massachusetts (1798); Cape Hatteras, North Carolina (1798); Ocracoke, North Carolina (1798); Gay Head, Massachusetts (1798); and Eaton's Neck, New York (1799).

This initial burst of construction was nearly complete when President George Washington died in 1799. Washington's insistence that lighthouse construction was made a national priority helped to create a more effective approach to manage and construct lighthouses along America's east coast.

# Fifth Auditor (1820)

In 1802, Albert Gallatin, the Secretary of the Treasury, resumed the responsibility for the aids to navigation. That responsibility was shifted back to the Commissioner of Revenue in 1818. In 1820 the fifth auditor was Stephen Pleasonton, a hard working auditor who remained at his post nearly 40 years and was known as the general superintendent of lighthouses. Because Pleasonton had very little nautical background, he relied on the professional experience of Winslow Lewis. In 1810, Captain Winslow Lewis persuaded the federal government to adopt the use of the Argand lamp with parabolic reflectors. Lewis' selling point was the lamps gave off a brighter light and used about one half as much oil. Lewis proposed to outfit all 49 lighthouses for a sum of $26,950. Right from beginning, the lights were inferior; it was noted through inspections and keepers' logs that the reflectors or mirrors which were silvered, the finish easily wore off. During the review by Stephen Pleasonton, the fifth auditor, he never identified this as problem to the Lighthouse Service.

# Lighthouse Board (1852)

Matters were getting worse. In 1847, Congress took action by taking away the construction of the lighthouses from the fifth auditor and placed it under the Army Corps of Engineers. In 1851, Congress authorized an investigating board consisting of two high-ranking Naval Officers, two officers from the Army Corps of Engineers, a civilian scientist and a junior officer of the Navy. In 1852, a 750-page report, critical of the Fifth Auditor, was presented to Congress. Congress proposed that the Lighthouse Board be created. The Board first met on October 9, 1852. Commodore Shubrick and his nine-member board had a huge job ahead to modernize all the lighthouses. (See The Fresnel Story.)

At first, the country was divided into 12 districts. The President assigned an army or naval officer as an inspector for each district. The Lighthouse Board moved quickly in applying new technology of installing Fresnel lenses, which were successfully used in European lighthouses. The Board created central depots, like Staten Island and Buffalo, to assist with inventory, dispatch, and repair of equipment. Over the next 50 years, the Board was mindful of advancing technologies and worked to install new types of lighthouses, buoys, or fog signals. Several of the new technologies included the Fresnel lens, the development of screw pile lighthouses, skeleton lighthouses, wave-swept interlocking lighthouses, iron caisson lighthouses, and breakwater lighthouses. Several advances in fog signals included the fog whistle, mechanically run clockworks, steam boiler whistles, steam boiler reed-trumpets, and bell signals. In 1886, a new technology was tested to illuminate the Statue of Liberty using electricity.

# Bureau of Lighthouses (1910)

In 1910, Congress wanted to give a civilian presence to the administration of the aids to navigation, abolish the U.S. Lighthouse Board. They created the Bureau of Lighthouses under the Department of Commerce. The Board hired a number of experienced civilians that took over the roles that the military officers had been fulfilling. President Taft appointed George R. Putnam to head the new agency as the Commissioner of Lighthouse Bureau. For 25 years, Putnam effectively led the Bureau and the number of aids to navigation increased substantially from 11,713 to 24,000. The increased aids were mostly buoys and small lights. In 1928, the first automated radio beacon was installed. With the installation of more automated lights, the Lighthouse Bureau staff was reduced by 800 employees.

In 1933, a photo-electric alarm device was developed to check the operation of unmanned lights. In 1934, a remote controlled lightship was equipped by the Lighthouse Bureau. By the 1920s and 1930s, the majority of the lighthouses had electric service, reducing the staff to operate the stations.

# Coast Guard

On July 7, 1939, the Lighthouse Service operations were transferred to the U.S. Coast Guard. Former Bureau Personnel were given the choice to remain civilians; about half chose to become members of the Coast Guard. During World War II, one of the many jobs of the Coast Guard was to guard the shores of the country. With the help of volunteers and career Coast Guard personnel, the Beach Patrol was formed to guard against enemy invasion, rescuing victims of German submarine warfare, and retrieving drowning victims. Some of the new technologies developed by the Coast Guard during and after the World War II were radio technology called SHORAN (short-range aids to navigation) and LORAN (long-range aids to navigation). By the end of World War II, the Coast Guard staffed 468 light stations.

In 1962, there were still 327 manned stations, despite the Coast Guard's effort to remove keepers from isolated stations. In 1968, they initiated the Lighthouse Automation and Modernization Program (LAMP). The LAMP program was designed to accelerate and standardize the remaining lighthouses for automation. Over $26 million was spent on LAMP over 20 years through 1989. The estimated annual savings was about $7 million. By 1990, all lighthouses but one, the Boston Harbor Island in Massachusetts, were automated.

The Coast Guard soon encountered a rising grassroots concern over the preservation of these old stations and many historical societies expressed a strong interest in obtaining a station to preserve and keep open to public. The Coast Guard set up a process for leasing the stations to local historical groups. Also many of the preservation groups, who have been successful in preserving lighthouses, have been given ownership of the lighthouses and the surrounding property.

# Three – Engineering, Architecture, and Physics of Lighthouses

The technologies used in the design and construction of lighthouses were part of an evolutionary process that began in the industrial revolution. Many design processes developed during the Industrial Age assisted engineers, architects, and contractors in building the lighthouses throughout America. Several styles of fuel-burning lamps were patented prior to the discovery of petroleum in Pennsylvania. A French physicist, Augustin Fresnel, who designed a glass prism lens that focused and magnified light brilliantly, transformed the lighthouse community.

## Early Lights

The first lighthouses that predated those in America used wood as a fuel. These lights were perched on hillsides that faced seaward. Simple towers were constructed and wood fires were placed on top. For almost 2,000 years, wood was the only source of fuel for lighthouses. Around the beginning of the sixteenth century, when coal was discovered in Europe, it was used for fuel because it produced a light that the sailors preferred. At one time, experiments were done with candles, but the light given off was not as bright as coal. As early as 1759 in England, the Eddystone Lighthouse used an oil lamp that contained a flat wick. One of the shortcomings of this new lamp was the smoke it gave off, hazing over the glass interior of the lantern room. A lantern with a pan and four wicks was one improvement made in the 1790s that met with limited success. This lamp type was used at the Boston Lighthouse as the principal illuminant until 1812.

### Argand Lamp with Reflectors

The first major breakthrough in illumination was made in 1781, using a design that was perfected by Swiss chemist Aimé Argand. The Argand lamp burned oil in a wick between two concentric tubes, producing a circular flame with two sources of oxygen. A glass chimney provided constant air flow as it protected the flame from irregular breezes. This lamp burned more intensely, was smokeless, and the light output was equivalent to seven candles. In England they began to fit eighteen to twenty inch reflectors to the Argand lamp. The Argand lamp achieved a pinnacle of success in England and France.

Figure 3-1. First-Order Fresnel Lens – Cutaway View

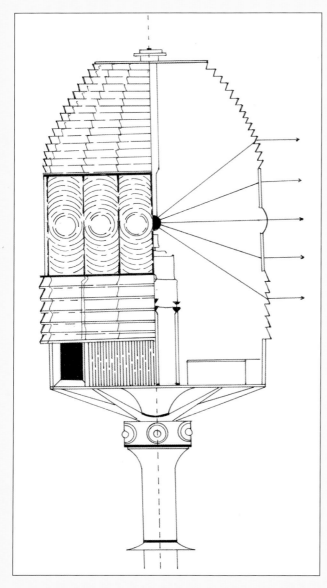

is capable of collecting 90% of the lamp's light and concentrating it into an intense horizontal ray. The lamps were designed in different sizes known as orders. The largest, known as a First-Order lens, was reserved primarily for tall coastal lighthouses such as Fire Island. Fixed lenses could be made to flash by placing a moving screen known as eclipsers in front of the optic. Some of the larger ordered lenses were divided into separate halves known as bivalve or clam shell lens. Table 1 shows the dimensions of seven different orders of Fresnel lenses.

| Order | Height | Inside Diameter |
|---|---|---|
| First | 7' 10" | 6' 1" |
| Second | 6' 1" | 4' 7" |
| Third | 4' 8" | 3' 3" |
| Third and 1/2 | 3' 0" | 2' 5 1/2" |
| Fourth | 2' 4" | 1' 8" |
| Fifth | 1' 8" | 1' 3" |
| Sixth | 1' 5" | 1' 0" |

Table 1 – Sizes of Fresnel Lenses by Order★
★Source: *Guardians of the Golden Gate: Lighthouses and Lifeboat Stations of San Francisco Bay*

## The Fresnel Lens

In 1822 Augustin Jean Fresnel (fray 'nel), a French physicist, introduced his magnification invention which changed the world. The lens was shaped like a giant beehive that surrounded a single lamp. The lens consisted of curved leaded-glass prisms that were supported by brass framework and arranged to apply the lenticular principles of physics. By positioning the prisms around the outside of the lens so that all the emerging rays are parallel to each other, the lens

Figure 3-2. Light Refraction in Fresnel Lens

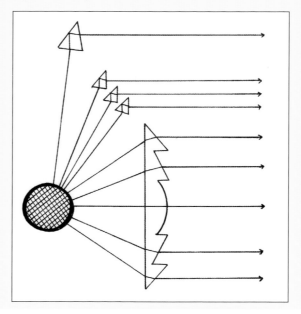

Today, the Coast Guard maintains 15 active landfall First-Order Fresnel lens. Block Island Southeast Lighthouse in Rhode Island is the closest First-Order light and is located east of Montauk Point. Depending on the weather, a First-Order lens which positioned at height of 100 feet is visible for up to 18 miles. These lenses could consist up to 1,000 prisms, stand up to 12 feet tall and weigh over three tons. They are valued at approximately $1 million dollars.

Figure 3-3. Original First-Order Fresnel Lens (1859) now in CapeMay County Historical Museum, Cape May, New Jersey.

## The Fresnel Story

Soon after the formation of the federal government, early management of the lighthouse system was placed in the U.S. Treasury Department. The Secretary of the Treasury administered lighthouses personally for several years.

Due to growing commerce, lighthouse operations required more time. As a result, the Commissioner of Revenue handled day-to-day management until 1802. Several transfers of responsibility of lighthouse system between the Secretary of the Treasury and Commissioner of Revenue took place between 1802 and 1820. In 1820, the lighthouse system became the responsibility of the Fifth Auditor of the treasury, Stephen Pleasonton. Pleasonton appointed local supervisors who handled all personnel matters, sites for lighthouses and other related structures, repairs to lighthouses, expenditures and inspections.

This administration had a variety of problems including Pleasonton's lack of technical and maritime experience. One example includes the time when Pleasonton wrote to France in 1830 to inquire about the Fresnel lens. After being informed of the cost, he decided they were too expensive and were not used. However, U.S. lighthouses did not meet with other countries' standards, so in 1838, major inspections were made on the U.S. lighthouse system. After these inspections, Congress passed an act in 1838 which divided the Atlantic Coast into six districts and the Great Lakes into two. Each district was inspected by a naval officer, where conditions of lights were found to vary from poor to good. Some of the worst conditions were due to substandard construction materials or techniques. Lightships were also in generally poor condition. Unfortunately no action was taken by Congress for years later.

Four years later, Congress appointed a committee to investigate the operation of several governmental departments and make recommendations. The committee concluded to take lighthouse duties from the fifth auditor and re-assign them to the Commissioner of Revenue. Due to criticism in the 1840s, Pleasanton and his lighthouse system came under investigation again in 1851. Starting in 1847, all new lighthouses constructed were placed under the review of the Corps of Engineers. In 1851, Congress authorized and required several civilian, naval and army engineers to investigate every aspect of the lighthouse system. This included construction, management, lighting, efficiency and comparing the U.S. system to other countries.

This investigation reported poor light quality and construction, lack of qualified keepers, defective lightships, and distribution of supplies was insufficient. Hence, the Board proposed a complete revamping of the system, including Fresnel lenses in all new lighthouses.

## Other Fuels

The fuel used in American lighthouses from the beginning was whale oil. Two strains of oil were used: a thick strain known as summer oil, and a thinner one for winter. In colder climates during the winter, thin oil tended to solidify, and it became necessary to keep a warming stove in the lantern room to maintain the proper viscosity of the oil. Sperm oil was used because it provided a high quality bright light. In 1855, sperm oil cost $2.25 per gallon up from 55 cents a gallon in 1840.

The Lighthouse Service began to look for a cheaper fuel. The French were using colza and rapeseed oil which was one-half the price of sperm oil. Rapeseed oil was obtained from wild cabbage. The government hoped to create a market but the farmers did not grow sufficient quantity to fill the needs of the lighthouse service. In the 1850s, the Lighthouse Service introduced colza oil, which within a few years, also proved to be insufficient.

Led by John Henry of the Smithsonian, a committee tested lard oil. Previous efforts had resulted in failure, but new tests showed that if the oil was heated to a higher temperature, it burned well. By 1867 lard oil was used exclusively in larger lamps. In the 1870s, test were made with kerosene or mineral oil. The tests were successful and in 1878 the Board introduced these fuels into Fourth-Order and smaller lenses.

The next change was in the source of the light, the incandescent vapor lamp. This lamp was similar to the Coleman lamp used by campers today. In this lamp, kerosene is forced into a vaporizer chamber where it strikes the hot walls and is instantly changed into vapor. The vapors go through a series of small holes to the mantle where it burns like a brilliant gas ball.

The final refinement was testing of electricity around 1900. Electricity was first used at the Statue of Liberty. Generators were gradually introduced in 1920s and 1930s to lighthouses where power lines did not reach. In addition, a multiple bulb holder moves a new bulb when an old one burns out was introduced. The use of electricity, coupled with a timer switch, eliminated many keepers' jobs. These automated procedures continued to reduce the work of the keeper.

## Engineering Designs

Most lighthouses can be categorized by the construction method, foundation type, and shape or building materials. Lighthouses can also be classified as land-based or aquatic. The major construction methods discussed here are wooden tower, masonry tower, wave-swept tower, concrete tower, cast-iron plate tower, skeletal tower, straight pile, screw pile, crib, caisson, breakwater, and Texas tower. The early lighthouse construction required solid rock or other stable foundation soils. In some locations a lighted buoy or lightship solved the problem. River and estuary environments, however, often had unstable muddy and sandy bottoms which could not support masonry towers. In the areas such as the Chesapeake Bay, Delaware Bay, the Gulf of Mexico, the Mississippi River delta, and the coral reefs of the Florida Keys, newer technologies were required. These included the screw pile, caisson, and skeletal tower type construction.

## Wooden Tower

Most early wooden towers have been burned or replaced; however at least 71 wooden towers still exist throughout the country. The Esopus Meadows lighthouse located near Kingston on the Hudson is one of few wooden towers that remain in New York State. Plymouth (Gurent Point) in Massachusetts is the earliest surviving wooden lighthouse.

Figure 3-4. Wooden Tower – Esopus Meadows, New York

## Masonry Tower

Masonry towers are constructed of rubble stone, cut stone, brick or concrete. Masonry is still the most popular lighthouse construction material. New York's oldest lighthouse, Montauk Point (1796), was built with dressed field stone that has stood the test of Atlantic Ocean surf for more than 210 years. The oldest standing masonry light tower in the United States is the Sandy Hook Lighthouse (1764) in New Jersey. It is 85-feet tall and built of cut stone. The tallest in the United States is the Cape Hatteras Lighthouse (1870) in North Carolina. It is 208 feet tall and constructed of brick. Fire Island Lighthouse (1858) on Long Island stands at 167 feet and is the tallest light in New York State. Fire Island is one of the 15 tall brick towers built along the Atlantic Coast.

Figure 3-5. Masonry Tower – Fire Island, New York.

## Wave-swept Tower

Wave-swept lighthouses, built on low rocks or submarine ledges, are constructed with interlocking stones to withstand the fury of waves and high seas during storms. The wave-swept lighthouse probably conforms to our mental image of the classical lighthouse than any other type. Only a few wave-swept towers have been built. One of the first wave-swept towers built in the United States is the 114-foot Minot's Ledge (1860), off the coast of Massachusetts. Preparing the foundation ledge took three years before the first course of stones were placed. Minot's Ledge is the most expensive lighthouse built in the United States at $300,000.

Figure 3-6. Wave-swept Tower – Eddystone, England

## Concrete Tower

Concrete towers began to replace brick masonry at the beginning of the twentieth century. The material was in many ways superior to iron and steel. It was cheaper, required less maintenance, and was extremely strong under forces of nature. Many lighthouses susceptible to earthquakes are made of reinforced concrete and are located mostly on the West Coast. The first reinforced concrete tower was built in 1910 at Point Areas, California. It stands 115-feet tall.

## Cast-iron Plate Tower

Cast iron is lighter than stone or brick, relatively inexpensive, strong, watertight, and deteriorates at a slow rate. In 1844, a cast-iron tower was built on Long Island Head in Boston Harbor. The earliest cast-iron lighthouses constructed in New York were Crossover Island (1882) and Rock Island (1882).

Figure 3-7. Cast-iron Plate Tower – Rock Island, New York

## Skeleton Tower

On-shore skeletal towers were first made of iron and later steel and typically were constructed on concrete foundations. The structure was pre-fabricated, taken to the construction site in pieces, and was similar to older style water towers. Offshore skeletal towers, also built of metal, were typically constructed with straight or screw-pile foundations. Whitefish Point Lighthouse (1861) and Manitou Island Lighthouse (1861), both located in Michigan and built from the same plan, are the earliest onshore skeletal towers. Coney Island Lighthouse is a good example of skeleton tower in New York State.

Figure 3-8. Skeleton Tower – Coney Island, New York

## Screw-pile

Alexander Mitchell invented the screw-pile and, with his son, patented their design in the 1830s. Mitchell combined his cast-iron design with wooden moorings and built the first screw-pile lighthouse in Lancashire, England in 1840. The screw anchor was fastened to the bottom of a wooden pile and was wound like a screw into the sand and silt. The Long Beach Lighthouse in New York's Gardiner's Bay is a good example of screw-pile design.

Figure 3-9. Screw-pile – Brandywine Shoals, New Jersey

## Straight-pile

Similar to the screw-pile lighthouse are the straight-pile skeleton towers. The pile foundation lighthouse utilizes the principal of least resistance. Waves can pass through rather than crash against the foundation. This design, used for offshore wave-swept locations, are built of cast-iron or wrought-iron piles and typically placed on mud or sandy bottoms. The earliest surviving straight-pile tubular skeletal tower is the Sombrero Key Lighthouse (1858) in Florida.

Figure 3-10. Straight-pile – Sombrero Key, Florida

## Wooden Crib

Wooden cribs are prefabricated onshore, floated and towed to the offshore site, and filled with stone to sink. This type was used extensively in the Great Lakes usually to replace lightships. Once the cribs are settled and leveled, they are usually capped with concrete or stone upon which the lighthouse structure is constructed. The most significant crib foundation lighthouses are the 93-foot Spectacle Reef Lighthouse (1874) on Lake Huron and the 110-foot Stannard Rock Lighthouse (1882), located on Lake Superior, 23 miles from the nearest land. Crib foundations are best suited for the hard rock bottoms found in the Great Lakes.

Figure 3-11. Wooden Crib – Spectacle Reef, Michigan

## Caisson

The ability to roll iron into large plates revolutionized the construction of lighthouses in northern bays and sounds. This method of construction reduced the cost of building a lighthouse foundation in the water. The hollow rolled-iron shell could be sunk up to 30 feet to the sea-bed floor and filled with sand, rock, or concrete. The caisson construction method for lighthouses is based on an idea developed by Lawrence Potts, an English physician and inventor. In 1845, he sank a section of hollow tubing to the ocean bottom and attached a powerful pump to the open end of the tube. The pump filled the tube with air and water was used to jet the caisson deeper into the sand bottom. This method was first used in 1850 in Rochester, New York, during the construction of bridge support towers. The first caisson lighthouse built in the United States was the Duxbury Lighthouse (1872) in Massachusetts. About 50 caisson-foundation lighthouses have been constructed in the United States.

## Breakwater

A breakwater is rock structure constructed offshore to dissipate wave energy as result of storm conditions. Sometimes lighthouses are constructed at the end of a breakwater, which is where they get their name. The majority of breakwater lighthouses are constructed on the Great Lakes. The breakwater lighthouse presents some unique challenges that were not solved until iron was introduced as a building material. The breakwater lighthouse had to be relatively light in order to avoid stress on the foundation. It also had to be strong in order to withstand the impact of waves, vibrations, and sometimes spring ice flows. Frequently, the keeper's quarters were in town because the breakwaters were too small to attach to the tower. An example of a breakwater lighthouse can be found in the Oswego Harbor, constructed in 1934 on the breakwater pier.

Figure 3-12. Breakwater – Oswego, New York

## Texas Tower

A relatively recent technological development in lighthouse construction is the Texas tower, which replaced the exposed lightships offshore. The Texas steel towers are an adaptation of the offshore oil drilling platforms first employed along the coast of Texas. The first Texas tower was the Buzzards Bay Lighthouse, Massachusetts (1961) which is now extinguished. Another example is the Ambrose Light Tower (1967) in New Jersey, which cost $2.4 million. It replaced the Ambrose Lightship and is now located in South Street Seaport in New York City.

Figure 3-13. Texas Tower

## The Lighthouse Generals

In 1852 the Lighthouse Service, composed of experienced military officers, engineers, and seamen, took charge of the Lighthouse Service. The Service immediately embarked on an ambitious program to expand and upgrade the navigation aids in America. Because the American economy was booming, Congress cooperated and provided funds to make these improvements. To accomplish the tasks the Service relied on the skills of two young military engineers, George Meade and Danville Leadbetter.

George Meade was trained as an engineer and graduated from West Point in 1835 at the age of 20. He was a surveyor for the Army Corps of Topographical Engineers and helped set the boundary between the United States and the Republic of Texas. Meade had an interest in marine engineering and lighthouses and began to work on towers in the Delaware Bay. Eventually Meade helped with some designs in the Florida Keys: Carysfort Reef (1850), Sand Key, and Sombrero Key.

Danville Leadbetter, an 1836 graduate of West Point, built lighthouses in the Gulf of Mexico. He preferred to use brick but also designed steel skeleton towers. In 1858 he completed a 200-foot tall tower at Sand Island off Alabama's Mobile Bay. Leadbetter oversaw the construction of Port Pontchartrain, built on a submerged concrete pad. His most unusual design was at Sabin Pass. This light was supported with a finlink foundation that spread weight over a larger area, and was built on damp yielding ground. It has remained in place for over 150 years.

With the outbreak of the Civil War in 1861, Meade rose quickly through the ranks to General of the Union Army. Meade fought in several key engagements while working his way to the rank of General. A string of key defeats of the Union Army on the Potomac had President Lincoln fire many generals. Meade was moved into this position in command on the eve of the critical battle of Gettysburg. Because of Meade's experience in Florida on building structures that could withstand storms, Meade built his defense on a series of hills overlooking Gettysburg. On the third and final day of the battle, when Lee released 13,000 men in Pickett's charge, his foundation held fast.

Leadbetter, joining the Confederate side, was in charge of Gulf coast fortifications and lighthouses. Because the Confederate naval force was weak, under Leadbetter direction, the Southern troops carefully removed and hid the Fresnel lenses to keep them out of the hands of the enemy. During the war, some key lighthouses were blown up; one such target was the Sand Island lighthouse which Leadbetter had built only a few years earlier.

# Four- Long Island

**Map 2. Long Island Lighthouses**

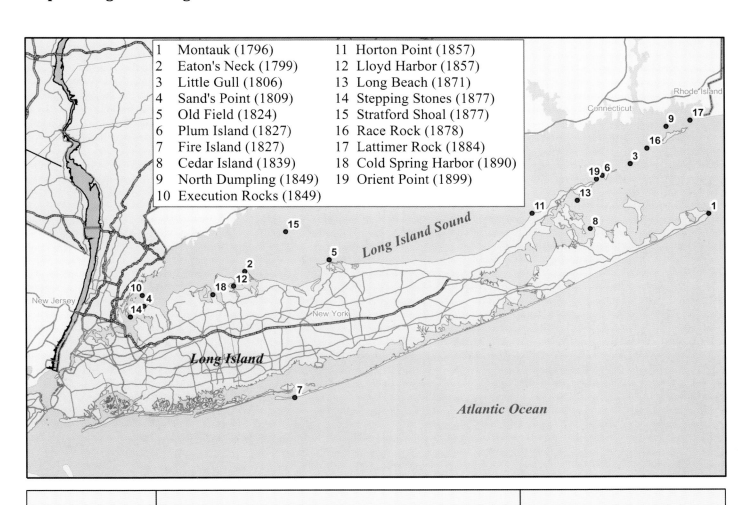

| | | | |
|---|---|---|---|
| 1 | Montauk (1796) | 11 | Horton Point (1857) |
| 2 | Eaton's Neck (1799) | 12 | Lloyd Harbor (1857) |
| 3 | Little Gull (1806) | 13 | Long Beach (1871) |
| 4 | Sand's Point (1809) | 14 | Stepping Stones (1877) |
| 5 | Old Field (1824) | 15 | Stratford Shoal (1877) |
| 6 | Plum Island (1827) | 16 | Race Rock (1878) |
| 7 | Fire Island (1827) | 17 | Lattimer Rock (1884) |
| 8 | Cedar Island (1839) | 18 | Cold Spring Harbor (1890) |
| 9 | North Dumpling (1849) | 19 | Orient Point (1899) |
| 10 | Execution Rocks (1849) | | |

**Long Island Lighthouses**

# Exploration and Colonization of Long Island

The history of Long Island is an integral part of the history of the United States. In 1524, an explorer named Giovanni DaVerrazano attached the first non-Indian names to large sections of Atlantic coastline from Georgia to Canada. He called the Hudson River region, "*Angoulême,*" which was the family name of the French king. He named Block Island, "Louisa Island," after the king's mother and he named his ship, "*Dauphne.*"

In April 1524, Verrazano and entered New York Harbor through a deep-cut channel between Staten Island and Long Island. He first began exploring the Hudson River in a smaller boat, where he encountered Indians in dug out canoes. He later returned to *Dauphne* and proceeded to Long Island. Verrazano had named this land *Flora*, but 84 years later, Henry Hudson, another explorer from the Netherlands, arrived in 1609 and gave it a Dutch name — *Lange Eylandt*.

In 1614, Adrian Block's ship, the *Restless*, was the first European vessel to travel up the East River through Hell's Gate on its way to Long Island Sound and eventually to Montauk Point. From Montauk, Block and his crew continued their voyage past an island, which would later be named Block Island. The early expeditions of Hudson and DaVerrazano were a result of these explorers seeking a more efficient route to the eastern Indian Ocean. Their motivation was to increase trade with India and China for their silk, spices, and gunpowder. Once they determined it was not possible to reach the Eastern Hemisphere via America, the colonization of Americas began in Long Island and Connecticut.

In 1638, Reverend John Davenport and Theophilus Eaton led the Puritans, who sought religious freedom from England, to Boston. These new Americans eventually settled in Connecticut on Long Island Sound near the Quinnipiac River, in a community they named New Haven. Within five years, four additional communities were founded in Connecticut and then Southold, New York, across the Long Island Sound. In 1659, Sam Wyllis acquired Plum Island from the Montaukett tribe. Plum Island is located just off Orient Point in Long Island Sound.

# Trade and Commerce

As each of the villages in Connecticut and New Amsterdam (Long Island) continued to grow along the Long Island Sound, docks or landings were built to provide mooring for boats that brought goods for trading or news from neighboring communities. Initially, surplus goods were traded by barter; Native America wampum, comprised of decorative strings or belts of seashells, was also used to pay for goods. In those days, merchants bought cattle, bacon, beaver skins, corn, and biscuits to sell to other areas on the Sound and in the bay area near Boston. In 1684, the British Crown granted permission to the colonies to begin roundtrip service from Boston to New York.

The Long Island Sound was an integral part of settling America in the 1600s, since it offered ships protection from the storms of the Atlantic and allowed small vessels to travel with great safety. However, unpredictable currents and tides were also responsible for shipwrecks. The *Prins Maurits* became the first of many shipwrecks on Long Island. It happened on March 9, 1657, in area known as South Beach, near the Fire Island Inlet. Since then, over 400 shipwrecks have been recorded in Long Island. Other famous wrecks include the *H.M.S. Colloden*, *H.M.S. Hussar*, *U.S.S. San Diego*, *U.S.S. Ohio*, and the *U.S.S. Turner*.

Figure 4-1. Montauk Point (1878)

# Montauk Point (1796)

Montauk Point is New York State's oldest lighthouse. It is located at the eastern tip of the South Fork on Long Island on a Native American site called Turtle Hill. Before settlers claimed this land, the Montaukett Indians used Montauk Point for signal fires. The lighthouse was ordered by George Washington and on April 10, 1795, it was proposed to the Revenue Office of the Treasury Department. John Macomb Jr., a bricklayer and architect, completed the 110-foot octagonal tower in 1796 at a cost of $22,300. The sandstone tower is six feet thick at the base and three feet at the top. Because of problems with the lamps, the tower was not lit or established until 1797. In 1860, 26 years before the French donated the Statue of Liberty, the French government donated a Fresnel lens to the United States, which was designated for the Montauk Lighthouse. The current light has a 2.5-million candlepower lamp that flashes white every five seconds and is visible for 19 miles.

In 1797, Montauk Point Lighthouse was 300 feet from the edge bluff. Erosion from waves and wind reduced the distance to 140 feet by 1930. Today, the lighthouse is only about 35 feet from the Atlantic Ocean! A number of attempts were made to stabilize the toe of bluff. In 1946, a 700-foot stone revetment was constructed using four to eight-ton stones, and built to a crest elevation of 23 feet. In 1972, the U. S. Coast Guard placed 280 linear feet of rock gabion baskets above the 1946 seawall.

In 1970, Georgiana Reid, a textile designer, came to Montauk with her husband, Donald, and developed a terrace system to stabilize the upper portion of the bluff. Reid won a prize for her systems design used to save the lighthouse. First timber terraces were installed. Then a common wetland plant, called Phragamites, was planted to secure the bluff. Reid organized work parties of volunteers, lasting over 15 years, in an effort to save the light. Some weekends, just Reid and her husband toiled in wind and rain to carry on this work. Again in 1992, the Montauk Historical Society constructed a new revetment.

By 2006, the U.S. Army Corps of Engineers and the New York State Department of Environmental Conservation completed a stability analysis of the bluff. They concluded that the existing revetment, constructed in 1992, would begin to fail within 15 years. They recommended the reconstruction of the 840-foot revetment using larger 12-ton stone at the base and increase the stone protection to a crest height of 40 feet.

In 1986, the Montauk Historical Society reached an agreement with the Coast Guard to convert the Montauk Point Lighthouse into a museum. The historic Montauk Point Lighthouse is the fourth oldest standing lighthouse in the United States. As a well-known landmark, it is widely used in corporate promotions and marketing campaigns throughout New York and United States. It is a popular tourist destination and site of weddings. Over 100,000 visitors travel to Montauk, where it remains a favorite spot for poets, writers, painters, photographers, and school children. The beautifully landscaped complex includes the original 1838 keepers house, double keepers dwelling, oil room, lighthouse tower, fog signal house, fire control station, and a newly constructed museum gift shop.

Montauk Point Lighthouse is a wonderful destination to anyone traveling to eastern Long Island. Just follow the signs passing through Montauk to the lighthouse.

Figure 4-2. Montauk Point and World War II Bunker (1970's)

Montauk Point – Montauk Point is New York State's oldest remaining lighthouse, completed in 1797.

Montauk Point – Turtle Hill – Once a Native American site, it is now owned by the Montauk Historical Society and is surrounded by 724 acres of state park land on the Montauk Point peninsula.

Montauk Point – Montauk Point is the fourth oldest active lighthouse in the United States.

Montauk Point – The current lighthouse lamp is equivalent to 2.5 million candle power.

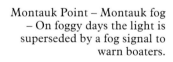

Montauk Point – Montauk fog – On foggy days the light is superseded by a fog signal to warn boaters.

Montauk Point – Fisherman's Memorial – A bronze and granite statue, located next to the lighthouse, was recently constructed to commemorate the lost fisherman of New York.

# Eaton's Neck (1799)

Located on the north shore in the Village of Asharoken, Eaton's Neck lighthouse is the second oldest lighthouse on Long Island. It was constructed by John MacComb Jr., architect and builder of Montauk Point, and was named after Theophilus Eaton. Eaton bought the land from the Matinecock Tribe, a local Indian tribe whose chief was Asharoken. Established on January 1, 1799, it is made of sandstone and shaped like an octagonal pyramid.

This lighthouse has undergone several renovations and repairs. Beginning in 1858, a Third-Order Fresnel lens was installed and in 1927 the Long Island Lighting Company added electricity. In 1871, a new fog signal was installed and in 1904 a newer fog warning system, an automatic siren, was installed. The Coast Guard automated the lighthouse in 1961.

Over 100 shipwrecks have occurred in the vicinity since 1790. The most famous shipwreck occurred in 1840 when the steamship *Lexington*, a 220-foot side-wheeler, which ran between New York and Connecticut, caught fire off the coast of Eaton's Neck. The *Lexington* carried 91 passengers, 39crew, and a cargo of cotton. The captain suffocated in the wheelhouse from the smoke and only four people were saved.

Currently, a large U.S. Coast Guard Station is located at Eaton's Neck, which includes ten buildings. In 1973, the Northport Historical Society was responsible for having the lighthouse listed in the National Register of Historical Places.

To get to the lighthouse, travel to the north shore of Long Island to the Village of Northport and through the Village of Asharoken to the Coast Guard Station, located on your right. Drive into the station and ask for permission to tour the grounds from the officer in charge.

*Right:*
Eaton's Neck – In 1638 Thaddeus Eaton and Rev. John Davenport led the Puritans to America, and eventually settled in Connecticut and Long Island.

Eaton's Neck – Over 100 shipwrecks occurred in this area of Long Island Sound, prior to the construction of the Eaton's Neck Light.

## United States Lifesaving Service

Thousands of lives have been saved from ships in distress along Long Island's shore since it was first settled in the seventeenth century. Some lives were saved by men in uniform from the Life Saving Service and some by private citizens. Sumner Kimball was given the daunting task of forming the United States Life Saving Service in 1871. Over the next seven years he molded the organization and was appointed by President Rutherford Hayes as the General Superintendent in 1878. The first stations were established in Hither Plain, Tiana, Forge River, Meadow Island, Jones Beach, and Far Rockaway in 1871. The motto of the Lifesaving Service was, "You have to go out but you don't have to come back!" In Long Island, there were a total of 30 stations built; 29 were along the Atlantic Ocean and one on Long Island Sound.

The cost of a first class coastal station was about $5,300. Each station had rescue equipment and apparatus to save lives. To rescue victims, surfmen rowed out in lifeboats, or used a Lyle gun to shoot line to stranded ships. After the line was fired by the lyle gun, a larger sturdier line was passed and tied off to a ship's mast. Early rescues were made with a life-car, which resembled a small boat with a top. The life-car, containing the rescued and crewmembers, was pulled ashore by surf-men. This rescue was painful, especially during high waves and storms. Later another technique was used for rescues. A breeches buoy, that shuttled one person at a time along a taught line above the water, was simpler and safer.

Most surfmen who risked their lives worked eight to ten months a year and earned $40 per month plus a meal allowance. This was eventually increased to $700 per year. The most productive life saving station in Long Island was Point O' Woods, averaging seven rescues per year. Over 7,000 lives were saved on Long Island by life stations on Fire Island alone. The brave men of the U.S. Life Saving Service (USLSS) saved an estimated 203,609 lives between 1871 and 1915. A total 285 life stations were built, equipped, manned, and maintained in the United States before the legacy was given to the Coast Guard on January 28, 1915.

1917 CGSTA #110, Island Beach (Seaside Park), N.J.

Ron Wilkins Photo.

L-R: Cale Worth, George Worth, Harold Wilkins, Edgar Sexton, Alvah Jones and Russel Penn.

Surfmen at the station were required to take a shift at daily watches. The watches were timed walks, which required the men to walk the beaches in opposite directions from the station. The stations were positioned four to six miles apart so the surfmen had to walk two to three miles, where were greeted by surfmen from the adjacent station.

Surfmen were required to maintain a uniform daily schedule, except for Sundays. Mondays were set aside for cleaning the station and equipment. Tuesdays' drills reviewed the use of the lifeboats. Wednesdays' drills were devoted to surfboats, beach apparatus, signals, and saving drowning victims. Thursdays' drills included the use of the beach apparatus, Lyle guns, and breeches buoys. Friday routines were practicing the restoration of the apparently drowned and other first-aid treatments. Saturdays were used for cleaning and washing. When the surfmen were not on watch, they shared in the cooking. Once every eight days, the men were given 22 hours of leave. Today in America approximately 115 life stations still stand as a monument of a great maritime era.

# Little Gull Island (1806, 1869)

Little Gull Island is situated seven miles northeast of Orient Point, at the eastern end of Long Island's North Fork, where Long Island Sound opens out to the sea. Great Gull Island is located just west of Little Gull Island, but four miles of open water lie between Little Gull Island and Fishers Island to the east. This stretch of water is known as the "Race," due to the tidal currents that sometimes exceed five knots. When strong winds or heavy onshore seas combine with an ebbing tide, the water in the Race turns into a churning caldron of white-capped waves and dangerous rip tides.

Along neighboring Plum Island, Samuel Wyllys purchased Little Gull Island in 1659 from Wyandanch, the senior chief of four Indian tribes who controlled much of Long Island at the time. Little Gull Island went through a number of owners until the U.S. government bought it in 1803 from Benjamin Jerome for $800.

Back in 1803, the island had one acre of land above the high-tide mark and rock reefs surrounding the island ensured that erosion would not be a problem. Almost all building materials were brought to the island by ship. The tower of the new lighthouse rose 53 feet above sea level and was made of smooth-hammered freestone. A wooden spiral staircase led to the lantern room. The one and a half story wooden keeper's dwelling had two rooms on the ground floor and a one-room loft upstairs, and was separate from the tower.

The first keeper at Little Gull Island was Israel Rogers. Rogers, along with his wife and children, and the assistant keeper and his family all had to share this small building in a location where they were sometimes isolated for up to two months at a time. This level of hardship and lack of privacy was typical for lighthouse personnel and their families. The next keeper was Israel's son-in-law, Giles Holt, who served an ultimatum to the local Superintendent of Lighthouses. Since the women would not put up with this arrangement any longer, and if an additional two bedrooms were not built, he would resign his post.

The station went into operation in 1805. Although the area was often covered with dense fog or haze, there was no fog signal at the station for another 51 years.

The War of 1812 began with a Declaration of War by the U.S. Congress. Communications were so slow in those times (it took four days for the news to reach Boston), and lighthouses were so remote, it is possible that Giles Holt may have not even known there was a war on, if it hadn't suddenly come to him. On July 28, 1813, a small British force landed at Little Gull Island. They did not destroy the lighthouse, but they took all the lamps and reflectors, putting the station out of service for the duration of the conflict.

Giles Holt and his family returned to the station after the war, but their routine was soon disrupted again when the great hurricane of September 23, 1815, came through New England. Little Gull Island was almost wiped clean. The lantern was ruined, all the windows were broken, the well was ruined, and outbuildings were demolished. Everyone at the station was forced to take refuge inside the lighthouse. One account says that when they emerged after the storm, they found the lighthouse sitting on a small patch of level ground sitting on a gravel bluff 20 feet high. Much of the island's soil around them had been washed into the sea.

Holt and his family were once again forced to leave the station while repairs were made. He returned without his family but resigned the following summer. Keeping the light in the family, his replacement was his nephew John Rogers II. Rogers was also the grandson of the first keeper, Israel Rogers. John Rogers kept the position for ten years, when he was fired for repeatedly letting the light go out.

A circular, eleven-foot-high stone wall was built around the station during the summer months of 1817. The wall had a diameter of 100 feet and was built to protect the station from future storms.

The station's first beacon was a multi-lamp/reflector combination powered by whale oil as was common in lighthouses of the day. Although that light was considered inadequate from the beginning, its replacement in 1837 by a similar optic with more lamps and larger reflectors was not much better. The original tower did finally receive a Fresnel lens of the third-Order, but by then plans were soon put in place for a new lighthouse on Little Gull Island.

In 1867, the Lighthouse Service began to erect the 81-foot gray granite tower that stands on the island today. The walls were five feet thick at the base and lined with brick. When it was finished two years later, the tower was attached to an impressive three-story keeper's house built of granite and wood. A Second-Order Fresnel lens was installed in the new tower and was exhibited for the first time on December 15, 1869. The light has been powered by whale oil, lard oil, kerosene, incandescent oil vapor and finally electricity in 1937.

In June 1926, the *Priscilla*, a paddlewheel originating in Fall River, Massachusetts, struck a ledge off Gull Island when it was on its way to Long Island. The impact of the crash caused the 560 passengers to fly out of their births and land on the deck. Miraculously, no serious injuries were reported.

The station was automated in 1978, ending 172 years of keepers on the island. Little Gull Light is still an active aid to navigation, casting a flashing white light over the area. The Fresnel lens was removed from the tower in 1995 and placed on display at East End Seaport Maritime Museum. The lighthouse grounds at Little Gull Island are not open to the public, but can be seen from the ferry that runs between Orient Point and New London, Connecticut.

Little Gull – The 81-foot granite tower is one of seven lighthouses in the Town of Southold.

# Sands Point (1809)

Although it is no longer an active light, Sands Point is located on the North Shore of Long Island, along the famous Gold Coast. Erected in 1809, it is the fourth oldest standing light tower on Long Island. Noah Mason was the builder and the first keeper until his death in 1841. The light was named after Captain John Sands (1649-1712), a skipper who sailed between New York and Virginia and was responsible for introducing locust trees to Long Island.

The original lamp burned whale oil, as most did in those days. The lighthouse signal was originally white with a one-minute flash, but it was changed to a fixed white light because it was confused with the signal of Execution Rocks, one mile north of Sands Point. The last keeper was Thomas J. Murray who served at Sands Point from 1917 until December 1922, when this light was no longer used as a warning beacon. The Government removed the lantern and replaced it with a flashing green light offshore in its place.

In the early 1900s Mrs. Belmont, who was a member of the prominent Vanderbilt family and owner of the Sands Point Hotel, purchased the property for $100,000 at a government auction. She also built the Beacon Towers on this property, which was a large mansion with fifteen master bedrooms. By 1927 she was broke and left the United States for France. William Randolph Hearst bought the property for $400,000 and his wife added a banquet hall and movie theater. The name was changed to Chateau St. Joan and was the inspiration of F. Scott Fitzgerald's *The Great Gatsby*. In 1937, they offered the property for $150,000 but there were no buyers. In 1940, the title was transferred to Dime Savings Bank as payment for the mortgage. The bank later leveled the mansion for $11,000 and the property was sold to Edmund Burke, who divided it into one-acre parcels for a housing development.

In 1968, a 38-foot tall steel tower was placed offshore on a reef north of the lighthouse. The lighthouse is located off of Sand's Point Road in the Town of North Hempstead. Today the original lighthouse tower sits on private land with only the original gates remaining. With the other buildings all gone, Sands Point is still a reminder to many of the opulent Gold Coast era, a colorful part of Long Island's rich history.

Sands Point – Erected 1809, the Sand Points Lighthouse served until 1922, when it was replaced with acetylene light on a pier. In 1927, William Randolph Hearst purchased the property and lighthouse, the name was changed to the Chateau St. Joan. It was the inspiration for F. Scott Fitzgerald's *The Great Gatsby*.

# Old Field (1824, 1868)

Located on a bluff near the entrance to Port Jefferson, the first light was established in 1824. It consisted of nine oil lamps with reflectors that burned whale oil. The tower was 30 feet tall and the lamp was at an elevation of 67 feet. The property to build the light was purchased from Samuel L. Thompson for $400 in 1823. The lighthouse only cost $2,980 to build. In 1830 when the first keeper, Walter Smith, died his wife, Elizabeth, assumed and retained the position of keeper for 26 years. Their daughter Mary continued as keeper from 1856 to 1868.

In 1868, a second lighthouse was constructed next to the existing light for $11,995. The new classically designed light was made of granite, with a circular glass tower, six feet in diameter. It sat above a two-story keeper's home. The first floor contained a kitchen, office and laundry area and the second had a full bath and three bedrooms.

In 1929, the Village of Old Field purchased the lighthouse for $2,405. During World War II, the Village was asked to vacate the lighthouse facility because it was needed for national defense. It became a base for a small Coast Guard contingent, which used it to spot aircraft. After the war, the property was returned to the Village.

This lighthouse has been the site of many amazing rescues. In 1923, Keeper Richard Ray rescued two men in a powerboat that drifted on a rock reef in front of the lighthouse. After rescuing the boaters, he provided them with dry clothing and shelter for next two days. In the late 1980s, Police Chief Robert Cummings and his family lived in the lighthouse.

In 1991, the Coast Guard replaced the lens in the tower with an alternating red and green flashing light. The keeper's house is currently the Village Hall and the Constable uses the original lighthouse building. The lighthouse can be viewed from Old Field Road which is north of the Village of Seatuaket.

Old Field – Old Field is a beautiful stone lighthouse that was erected in 1824 at the entrance to Port Jefferson Harbor.

*Right:*
Old Field – The rock revetment serves to protect the base of the shoreline bluff. The top of the bluff is 30 feet from the foundation of the Old Field Light.

Old Field – Today the keeper's house serves as Village Hall for the Town of Old Field. The original light is used as the Village Constable's Office.

Old Field – Old Field Lighthouse has a cast iron tower.

# Plum Island (1827, 1870)

In full view from Orient Point on the North Fork in Suffolk County, Plum Island Light is located 110 miles east of New York City. The 840-acre island is 2.9 miles long by 1.7 miles wide. Known by the early settlers as "Isle of the Patomos," explorers observed beach plums and hence the island was renamed Plum Island. Samuel Wyllys purchased the island from Wyandach, Chief of the Montauketts, on April 27, 1659. The original 1827 light consisted of ten oil lamps with reflectors. In 1859, it was refitted with a Fourth-Order Fresnel lens and 350,000-candlepower lamp, which could be viewed up to a range of 14 miles. Plum Island was often a stopping place for tall ships traveling into New York Harbor.

In 1870, a new Victorian-Gothic Revival lighthouse was completed with a Fourth-Order lens, revolving every 30 seconds. Will Chapell, who transferred from Long Beach Bar Light, was appointed the keeper in July of 1913. Chapell's eldest daughter Elsie married the keeper of the adjacent Orient Point Light.

In 1930, the Department of Justice considered using the island for a maximum-security prison. In 1956, the Army closed Fort Terry and turned the island over to U. S. Department of Agriculture for an animal disease research center. Currently the USDA employs over 300 people who take a private ferry from Orient Point to Plum Island to work.

In June 1978, the light was discontinued and was replaced with a flashing white light, located on a brick shed near the lighthouse. Recently the Army Corps of Engineers placed rock near the original lighthouse to prevent erosion along the buff on west side of the island. The Plum Island lighthouse can be viewed from Orient Point State Park or while traveling on the Orient Point to New London, Connecticut ferry.

Plum Island – The current design is similar to the Old Field Light and was established in 1827. Today USDA owns and operates an animal disease research facility on the island.

# Fire Island (1827, 1858)

Prior to the Statue of Liberty, the Fire Island Lighthouse was the first glimpse of the American Dream many saw before arriving in New York Harbor. The first tower, constructed in 1827, was an 85-foot octagonal tower that cost $10,000 to construct. The original tower was located due east of the dangerous Fire Island Inlet. This lighthouse was the site of many shipwrecks. On July 19, 1850, the *Elizabeth* went aground near the community of Point O' Woods. Margaret Fuller, the first women journalist, was one of the ten people who lost their lives in this accident.

A new 167-foot circular tower was constructed in 1858, 200 yards northeast of the existing towers. This new tower was comprised of 800,000 bricks and was painted yellow. Sailors affectionately called Fire Island "the winking woman" because the lighthouse resembled a statuesque lady in a long yellow dress. In 1971, the exterior of the lighthouse was resurfaced with Portland cement and painted with black and white bands. An electric generator was also installed, making the lamp electrified for the first time in its history.

In 1974, the beacon on top of the Robert Moses State water tower took over the task of signaling ships and Fire Island was extinguished. In 1981, the National Park Service acquired the Fire Island Lighthouse and the Fire Island Lighthouse Preservation Society was formed the next year. The Preservation Society worked towards relighting the tower and establishing environmental, historical and education programs.

Today the lighthouse is one of the jewels of the Fire Island National Seashore. The Barrier Island, on which it sits, has grown and now extends more than 3.5 miles to the west due to the shifting sands on the South Shore. To visit the lighthouse, drive to Robert Moses State Park. Park in Field 5 and follow the signs along a short boardwalk. Artifacts from the U.S. Lifesaving Service (USLSS) and historical maps can be found in the lighthouse museum.

Fire Island – To access the Fire Island Lighthouse there are a series of paths and boardwalks.

Fire Island – The current Fire Island is the tallest lighthouse in New York state. Constructed with 800,000 bricks, it stands 167 feet tall.

Fire Island – In 1971, the exterior of Fire Island Lighthouse was resurfaced using Portland cement and was painted with black and white bands.

Fire Island – The Fire Island Lighthouse is a great destination to play on the white sandy beaches and to the view wildlife of Long Island.

Fire Island – In 2007, the First Order Frensel lens was returned to the Fire Island Lighthouse Society after being displayed and stored at the Franklin Institute of Science for nearly fifty years. A permanent exhibit space will be constructed to display the lens.

# Cedar Island (1839, 1868)

In 1736, the Town of East Hampton built the road to Cedar Island Lighthouse; it was later widened in 1795. On August 13, 1838 the Town sold the property to the U.S. Government for $200. This island had approximately 50 cedar trees, which is where Cedar Island got its name. Located at the tip of Cedar Point Park, the 32-foot wooden lighthouse was built for $3,480. Cedar Island was illuminated by nine 14-inch reflector lamps and had a range of 12.5 miles. Originally, it was a guide for whaling ships entering Sag Harbor between Northwest Harbor and Gardiner's Bay.

In 1868, a new 35-foot tall, 2.5-story lighthouse was constructed southwest of the existing tower. The new tower contained a Sixth-Order lens; an automated fog bell was added in 1882. Similar to the Saugerties Lighthouse, which is on the Hudson River, the new building was constructed of Vermont granite. In 1904 and 1906, 6,000 tons of rock riprap was placed to protect the island. Later in 1908, a breakwater was constructed to protect the shoreline. In 1923, the yacht *Florence Simmons* sank near the island; all four crewmembers were saved.

This light changed hands several times in its history. In 1934, the lighthouse was turned over the U.S. Treasury Department, was decommissioned, and a steel skeleton tower was erected. In 1937, the lighthouse and one acre of land were auctioned in Manhattan for $2,002. W. Bettie of Fall River, Massachusetts, made the purchase. In 1943, it was sold to Isabelle Bradley, who had been renting from Beattie for four years. As a result of the 1938 hurricane, a 200-yard sandbar formed connecting the island to mainland. In 1967, Bradley sold the property and the lighthouse to Suffolk County Parks.

After a fire, in 1974 it was discovered that the insurance on the property had lapsed. Sag Harbor Whaling Museum then approached Suffolk County to restore the lighthouse and eventually raised $100,000 to restore the roof. In 2004, the lighthouse was listed on the National Historic Register. Today, Cedar Island Lighthouse is a priority for restoration and is wonderful location for swimming, fishing, and boating. The lighthouse is part of Cedar Point County Park and is located off Old Northwest Road in the Town of East Hampton.

Cedar Island – The Cedar Island Light was established in 1839 to assist vessels navigating Sag Harbor, which was a busy whaling community in the early 1800s.

# North Dumpling (1849, 1871)

North Dumpling Lighthouse, a red brick two-story lighthouse, was constructed and established in 1849. The lighthouse was illuminated with seven 14-inch reflector lamps with red shades. It is located on a small island adjacent to Fisher's Island in the Fisher's Island Sound. John Winthrop, Jr., the governor of Connecticut, originally purchased the island from the Pequot Indians. In 1847, William Winthrop sold the island to the U.S. government for $600. Riley Clark was appointed the light's first keeper on October 18, 1848, but never reported for duty. Joseph Dayton, a local sea captain was temporarily placed in the position.

In 1856, a fog bell was added and a 270-degree Sixth-Order Fresnel replaced the reflector lamps. In 1861, Joseph Totten recommended some repairs to the lighthouse. Totten was well respected and known for his construction of forts and lighthouses. One of the famous American lighthouses that Totten engineered was Minot's Ledge, just off Boston Harbor. In 1871, a new 70-foot lighthouse was constructed and established and the keepers' quarters and a new barn. In 1900, the Lighthouse Board granted permission to the Southern New England Telephone Company to construct a telephone plant at the lighthouse.

Fisher's Island has a rich and colorful history. During Prohibition in the 1920s, residents at Fisher's Island were involved in bootlegging alcohol. In 1938, a severe hurricane caused considerable damage to the island, especially the lighthouse. The bell tower, boathouse, and storehouse were all destroyed by this storm. In 1959, the Coast Guard automated the light, erected a steel tower on the southwest section of the island, and put the lighthouse up for auction. George Washburn bought the island for $18,000 and resold it in 1980 to David Levitt for $95,000, who rebuilt it. In 1986, the island and lighthouse changed hands again and was sold to Dean Kemen. The lighthouse can be viewed traveling on the ferry from Orient Point to New London, Connecticut.

North Dumpling – The beautiful red brick North Dumpling Lighthouse is located on a private island adjacent to Fisher's Island in Block Island Sound.

# Execution Rocks (1849)

Located off the rocks of Sands Point at the western end of Long Island Sound, Execution Rocks is a 60-foot tower with 13 reflector lamps. Thomas Butler completed it in May 1849. No one knows exactly how this lighthouse got its name. Some say that during the Revolutionary War, the British took captured prisoners to the island, chained them to rocks during low tide, and the prisoners perished during the rising tide. Most likely, the lighthouse was named after the term "execution," which was the word to describe the outcome of many ships crashing on the rocks and shoals in this area. This was the story cited in Frederick Van Wyck's *"Recollections of an Old New Yorker."*

In 1856, a new Fourth-Order lens was installed with a fixed white light, which was visible for 12 miles. In May 1873, Charles Sherman was appointed as keeper. His wife Mary joined him as one of two assistant keepers shortly thereafter. Charles and Mary remained at Execution Rocks until June 1882. Mary was one of five assistant women keepers. The other female keepers in the late 1800s were Alicia Odell (1859), Clarissa Miller (1867-1869), Jane Williams (1869-1871), and Ellen Farser (1871).

The storms on Long Island Sound were treacherous and made life on the tiny island a challenge. In order to increase the protection the island from 1870 to 1902, approximately 1,900 tons of rock riprap was placed. On February 4, 1920 the steamer *Maine*, an early screw-propeller passenger ship, ran aground at Execution Rocks. In 1915 and in 1918, the engine house caught fire. Fortunately, no lives were lost.

In 1921, assistant keepers Walter Story and Leonard Hainsworth were given service commendations for saving the lives of two men who had capsized in a sudden windstorm. As part of a routine inspection in 1966, the Coast Guard described the lighthouse as a white light that is 600,000-candle-power, flashing every ten seconds, and standing 62 feet above sea level. In 1979, the lighthouse was automated after the Fresnel lens was removed and replaced with a modern beacon which flashes every four seconds. The lighthouse is only accessible by water but is visible from several points in New Rochelle, on the north shore of Long Island.

Execution Rocks – A clear calm day in Long Island Sound with many gulls and black cormorants perched on the rocks.

# Horton Point (1857)

George Washington stopped at Horton Point in 1757 on his way to Boston. He proposed that a lighthouse be built, but it was not constructed until 1857. Horton Point was named after Barnabus Horton who landed in 1640 at Founders Landing Road, at the foot of Hobard Road in Southold. Congress appropriated $4,000 in 1854 for Horton Point Lighthouse.

A Federal-style lighthouse, with two stories and an inviting porch, it is perched on a cliff 103 feet above Long Island Sound. Horton Point has a Third-Order Fresnel lens with a green light flashing every ten seconds and is visible for 20 miles.

William Sinclair was appointed as the first keeper at a salary of $400. In September 1896, Robert Ebbitts, who served in the 127th Regiment from New York during the Civil War, was assigned keeper. He served as master of several coastal vessels and joined the Lighthouse Service. During his tenure with the Lighthouse Service, Ebbetts served as assistant keeper at Plum Island, keeper at Cedar Island, and keeper at Horton Point. Ebbetts remained at Horton Point until 1919 when he was replaced by George Erharrdt, the last Keeper. In July 1933, the Horton Point Lighthouse was extinguished and replaced with a 40-foot steel skeletal tower.

On December 10, 1937 the 7.62 acre site was conveyed to the Town of Southold. On January 2, 1942, the U.S. Coast Guard notified the Town of Southold that the site would be used for naval defense for the war. After the war, it was abandoned for many years. A nautical museum opened in 1977 at the keeper's quarters. In 1990, the tower was repaired, a new FA-251 optic was installed, the skeletal tower was demolished, and the Coast Guard donated a new flagpole in place of the tower. The porch was refinished in 1993 and in 1994 the Hor-

ton Point Lighthouse was placed on the National Register of Historic Places. To view the lighthouse in Southold, travel east on County Route 48. Turn left (north) on to Lighthouse Road and follow the signs to the lighthouse. The museum at the lighthouse has an excellent collection of maritime and nautical artifacts.

Horton Point – George Washington wanted to have a lighthouse constructed at Horton Point, but it was not until 1857 that a lighthouse was established.

# Lloyd Harbor (1857, 1912)

In 1838, George Bache recommended that a small beacon be erected at the entrance to Lloyd Harbor, to assist ships entering Huntington Bay. It was not until 1854 that Congress appropriated $4,000 to construct a lighthouse on the South Point of East Beach. The 34-foot tall brick tower had a Fifth-Order lens from a white light that was projected at an elevation of 48-feet above sea level.

Since the station was damaged by a large storm on November 2, 1870, a granite seawall was constructed the following spring to reduce the wave attack on the lighthouse. This was the first of several attempts to address the vulnerability of the lighthouse to storm damage. The seawall was damaged by ice in 1872 and in 1875, additional rock was placed around the lighthouse.

A new lighthouse and fog signal were placed into service on June 16, 1912, at a cost of $32,551. The new foundation consisted of a 26 by 30-foot reinforced concrete crib that was floated and sunk in position. Riprap was placed around the sunken crib to shore up the foundation. A concrete dwelling that contained a sitting room, kitchen, bedroom, and lighthouse tower was built 31-feet above sea level. A Fifth-Order lens, with a flashing red lamp that was visible for eight miles, was installed in the tower and a 1,000-pound bell, rung by a No. 4 fog-bell striker, was placed on the lighthouse deck. On June 26, 1924, the old Lloyd Lighthouse and 2.5 acres of property were deeded to the State of New York and eventually transferred to the Town of Huntington. The Lloyd Harbor Light was renamed the Huntington Harbor Lighthouse.

Art Bouder along with his wife, Harriet, and son moved into the Lloyd Harbor Lighthouse in 1935. Art Jr., greatly influenced by his dad, decided on a career in the Coast Guard and was stationed in 1953 at the Eaton's Neck facility. One of Art Jr.'s noteworthy rescues was saving Professor Albert Einstein and his lady friend, whose sailboat capsized not far from the Coast Guard facility.

In 1949, the massive concrete lighthouse was automated and in 1967, the Coast Guard issued a notice to remove the light from service. Because of local protest, the light was continued. In 1985, the Coast Guard also considered demolishing the light but a local citizens group formed the "Save Huntington Lighthouse" coalition to stop the Coast Guard. The Coast Guard leased the property to the coalition, which changed its name to the Huntington Lighthouse Preservation Society in 2003. This group was responsible for having the lighthouse placed on the National Register of Historical Places in 1989. The lighthouse can be seen from Huntington Harbor off Lighthouse Point Road in West Neck.

*Right:*
Lloyd Harbor – The original lighthouse was erected in 1857 at the entrance to Lloyd Harbor to assist ships entering Huntington Bay. The Huntington Lighthouse Preservation Society was responsible for saving the lighthouse and placing it on the National Register of Historic Places in 1989.

# Long Beach (1871, 1990)

In 1868, the Lighthouse Board received a petition for a beacon at the entrance to Peconic Bay in the Town of Southold. In 1870, Congress appropriated $17,000 for the lighthouse that would come to known as "Bug Light." Plans were drawn for a 2.5-story wood lighthouse on a screw-pile foundation and work was completed in the fall of 1871.

On November 25, 1871, the final touches were made at the Long Beach Bar Lighthouse the lighting of a fixed red lamp with a Fifth-Order Fresnel lens. In 1872, Congress appropriated an additional $20,000 for granite blocks to be placed around the base and serve as icebreakers.

The 1946 Light Lists reported that Long Beach had an 870-candlepower fixed red light with a Fourth-Order Lens. After the Commander of the Third District had declared Long Beach Bar "excess property," the General Services Administration recommended that the lighthouse be auctioned. The auction was announced in the November 3, 1955, issue of *News Review*. The Orient Marine Association, who had the highest bid, purchased the lighthouse in February 1956. On July 4, 1963, arsonists burned the abandoned structure and the 91-year-old Long Beach Bar was destroyed. In the 1980s, a replica of the original light was proposed and in September 1990 that dream was fulfilled. Today the East End Seaport Museum and Marine Foundation maintain the lighthouse, while the Coast Guard cares for the light. Bug Light is the only lighthouse on Long Island where guests can stay overnight. Two primary vantage points to view Bug Light are from Shelter Island, along Ram Island Drive, and from the south off Route 25, just east of East Marion. There is large bronze plaque on a huge stone along Route 25, near East Marion, so visitors can find the lighthouse.

Long Beach – Also known as "Bug Light," Long Beach was rebuilt in 1990 after a fire in 1963. Bug Light is the only lighthouse on Long Island which welcomes overnight guests.

# Stepping Stones (1877)

Stepping Stones is the western most lighthouse on Long Island's North Shore. It is located just east of the Throg's Neck Bridge. Known by Native Americans as the "Devil's Stepping-Stones," the lighthouse was constructed on a boulder reef and lit on March 1, 1877. Because of the high volume of maritime traffic leaving the East River and entering Long Island Sound, it was necessary that these rocks be marked. Stepping Stones Lighthouse has a sister light, the Hudson Athens Lighthouse, which was also constructed from same plans.

Findlay Fraser was appointed as the first keeper and remained until July 15, 1879. Ernest Bloom who became keeper in 1910 was awarded the Lighthouse Service Efficiency Pennant in 1911. On July 28, 1921, keeper Stephen Holm rescued two men whose canoe had overturned near the lighthouse. Again on July 18, 1923, Holm rescued two men whose sailboat ran aground on rocks at Stepping Stones. The original lens was upgraded in 1932 from a Fifth-Order lens with fixed red light to a Fourth-Order fixed green light. In 1968, the Stepping Stones Lighthouse was automated with a 1,700-candlepower green light that flashes every four seconds. The lighthouse can be viewed from the Throg's Neck Bridge or from the U.S. Merchant Marine Academy in Kings Point.

Stepping Stones – This light was constructed from the same plans as the Hudson-Athens Lighthouse. Today the automated light flashes green every four seconds.

# Stratford Shoal (1877)

When Adrian Block made his exploration voyage of Long Island Sound in 1614, he charted two islands where Stratford Shoal light now stands. The Stratford Shoal Light, similar to Execution Rocks, stands guard over a dangerous offshore area between New York and Connecticut on the Long Island Sound. Before the permanent light was constructed at Stratford Shoal, Congress appropriated $10,000 in 1837 for a light-ship. A 100-ton white oak vessel was built in Norfolk, Virginia. In January 1838, one of the earliest light ships was stationed Stratford Point. In 1872, the Third District Engineer asked to replace the lightship with a lighthouse because it would be more durable and economical.

Work began in 1873 and expenditures through 1878 totaled $140,000. On December 15, 1877, the light was lit. William McGloin was transferred from a lightship to the lighthouse and was named the first keeper. The dwelling, which accommodated one keeper and two assistants, had a kitchen, sitting room, living room, and five bedrooms. A Fourth-Order lens was operated by a clock-work mechanism, similar to what is used in a household grandfather clock.

To protect the light from the high seas and storms, an additional 1,900 tons of rock riprap were placed around the station between 1895 and 1902. On November 12, 1912, the light was changed from oil to a 40,000-candlepower, incandescent oil vapor lamp. A radio beacon was established at Stratford Shoal in March 1927 and the light's signal was one dot, two dashes, and one dot.

On May 5, 1921, Keeper Henry McCarthy and Assistant Keeper John Horlacher were commended by the Lighthouse Service for aiding a crew whose boat had been blown up on the rocks due to a strong gale.

In August 1970, the Stratford Shoal Light was automated and today the light can viewed when crossing the Long Island Sound on the ferry from Port Jefferson to Bridgeport, Connecticut.

Stratford Shoal – This light is similar to Execution Rocks. It stands guard over a dangerous offshore area between New York and Connecticut n Long Island Sound. In 1895 and 1902, a total of 1.9 thousand tons of rock riprap were placed around the lighthouse to protect the foundation.

# Race Rock (1879)

Race Rock, eight miles from New London, Connecticut, has always been a treacherous place for mariners. It is located at the western end of Fisher's Island. Early records show that Race Rock was marked by buoys prior to 1745.

Constructing this lighthouse was a major engineering marvel. The foundation took six years to build because the construction surface was 3 to 13 feet below sea level. The project foundation required 10,000 tons or 20 million pounds of rock. The Gothic Revival lighthouse is constructed of stone with a tower height of 40-feet above Long Island Sound. It included accommodations for a keeper and two assistants. In the basement is a pantry and cool closet, and on the first floor are two kitchens, dining rooms and sitting rooms. On the second floor are five bedrooms and a spiral staircase that leads to the lantern room. Race Rock was completed in 1878.

Thomas and Scott Smith engineered and aided in the construction of the lighthouse. Frances also built the seawall at Governor's Island, which is on the East River and the seawall at Liberty Island, which are both in New York City. Over the course of history, many ships and lives were lost in the vicinity of Race Rock. In November 1846, the steamer Atlantic slammed into the rocks and 45 passengers and crew perished. In 1922, because of an inoperative fog signal, the steamer *Arizona* was grounded at the station. Several years later, the barge Victorious broke away from its tug and hit the rocks around Race Rock. Keeper George Tooker, and his assistants Ernest Witty and Emanuel Weber, rescued Captain Hazell who found himself in imminent danger. All received commendations from the U.S. Department of Commerce for the rescue, which was accomplished in very hazardous condi-

tions. The lighthouse was automated in 1978 and flashes red every ten seconds. The lighthouse can be viewed from either the Orient Point or Block Island ferries.

Race Rock – Construction of Race Rock was an engineering marvel. It took six years just to build the foundation, which was three feet below sea level. The 67-foot Gothic Revival structure was the last of the offshore masonry-style lights. Later construction practices were changed to less expensive caisson lights, such as Latimer Reef or Orient Point.

# Lattimer Reef (1884)

The Lattimer Lighthouse was named after John Latemore, who set out during the War of 1812 to spy on a British fleet at Fisher's Island. Latemore was captured and hanged by the British after his skiff ran aground.

It is not certain how the reef was named, but it may have been named after the Latimer family, who lived in New London, Connecticut, in the 1660s. Robert Latimer worked in the coasting trade as a partial owner of the bark Hopewell. A 13-foot tall iron spire marked the reef with a white vane on top of Latimer Rock. In the nearby waters of Connecticut, a lightship was stationed at Eel Grass Shoal in 1849. Several lightships replaced this one between 1871 and 1877. Located at the east end of Fisher's Island, the Latimer Reef Lighthouse was built to replace the Eel Grass Shoal Lightship. The Latimer Reef Lighthouse is made of cast iron and its base is 30 feet in diameter. On top of the base was a 21-foot tower that contained three floors and a watch deck. Above the tower was the lantern structure that held the Fifth-Order lens with flashing white lamp. The lamp was first lit July 1, 1884, and the first keeper was Charles Noyes, who had been the master on the Eel Grass Lightship.

In 1907, the lighthouse exhibited a flashing white light every ten seconds from its Fourth-Order lens. A bell was struck every 15 seconds in foggy weather.

During the 1938 hurricane, the Lighthouse Service Bulletin identified Latimer Reef as one of the stations at which "principal damaged occurred." The hurricane destroyed small boats, power lines, and caused damage to the foundation, windows and doors. In 1983, a 300-mm lens replaced the Fourth-Order lens and in 1997, the tower was painted with white and brown stripes. Today, Latimer Reef has the distinction of being the oldest cast-iron lighthouse in the First District of the Coast Guard. It can be seen from the Block Island Ferry.

Latimer Reef – The Latimer Reef Light was built to replace the Eel Grass Shoal Lightship and is the oldest cast-iron lighthouse in the U.S. Coast Guard's First District.

# Cold Spring Harbor (1890)

Figure 4-4. Cold Spring Harbor

Similar to Sag Harbor, Cold Spring Harbor was well known for its fleet of whaling ships in the 1800s. Whale oil was a highly prized resource for lighting, and the whaling community of Cold Spring, diligently worked to build the largest and fastest whaling vessels. The first effort to build a lighthouse in Cold Spring Harbor was noted in the Lighthouse Board's Annual Reports (1876–1878). Plans were drawn up for a cast iron tower in 1879. Since problems arose over purchasing the land for the lighthouse, it wasn't until June 1889 that a final proposal was accepted.

The light was established on January 21, 1890, and William Keen was assigned as the first keeper. The station had a fixed white light with a red sector, which was positioned 40 feet above sea level. A fog signal that was struck by machinery every 30 seconds complimented the Cold Spring Harbor Light.

In the early 1900s, Arthur Jensen was the keeper at Cold Spring. He had the honor of welcoming President Theodore Roosevelt several times. Sagamore Hill, Roosevelt's summer White House was nearby and Roosevelt would often visit by rowboat with his children.

In the 1940s, the light was upgraded to an incandescent oil-vapor lamp and Fourth-Order lens, producing a 2900-candlepower beam of white light. The light was fully automated in November 1948. In 1965, the wooden tower was removed from the cast iron foundation. After a local woman expressed interest in buying the lighthouse, it was sold to her for one dollar. Today Cold Spring Harbor is the only lighthouse on Long Island that has been relocated and is privately owned. A skeletal tower replaced the wooden structure on top of the cast iron caisson.

Cold Spring Harbor – President Teddy Roosevelt and his family often rowed out to the lighthouse, from his nearby home on Sagamore Hill. The upper wooden portion of the Cold Spring Lighthouse was purchased and placed at a private residence on the North Shore of Long Island.

# Orient Point (1899)

Known as the "coffee pot" because of its shape, Orient Point was constructed to replace the Oyster Ponds Reef Lightship that was destroyed in 1872. It was lit November 10, 1899, and manned by Ole Anderson, who was paid only $600 per year.

It is located at the tip of Long Island's North Fork, between Gardiner's and Peconic Bays. This area is also known as Plum Gut because of the strong rip tide between the two bays. The shell of the foundation is a 25-foot diameter cast iron caisson. The focal height of lighthouse tower is 64 feet and it contains a Fifth-Order lens. Around the base of the light, 600 tons of rock riprap were deposited to prevent erosion. In 1902, the Lighthouse Board decided additional storm protection was needed and an additional 9,000 tons of rock were placed.

In the 1920s, William Chapel, the keeper of the Plum Island Lighthouse, also took care of Orient Point. Chapel had three daughters and a son, Willie, who later became keeper at Orient Point. Willie had an assistant named Bill Baker. Baker fell in love with Willie's sister, Elsie, were married and moved to Medford.

Because of the location of Orient Point in the Sound, it was key in saving lives. On September 6, 1936, Keeper Marvin Andrews used his motorboat to rescue three persons aboard a sloop. Andrews received commendations from the Secretary of Commerce for his bravery. By 1966, the station was fully automated but in 1970, the Coast Guard announced plans to demolish the lighthouse. The Coast Guard proposed to remove the tower with explosives and replace the light with a reinforced pipe tower with day marks. After public outcry the plans were delayed. In 1973 work began to repair the aging tower by sandblasting, patch holes with plugs, and painting the tower with epoxy-based paint. Today the light flashes every five seconds and many riders of the Orient Point to New London ferry view the revitalized lighthouse. The lighthouse can also be seen from the most eastern point on the North Fork, just past the ferry terminal parking at the County Park. The best access to the point is by walking or biking.

Orient Point – This light is known as the "coffee pot," because of its shape. It is located in Plum Gut, where Long Island Sound meets Gardiner's Bay.

Orient Point – The swiftly moving waters of Plum Gut make this area a great spot for fishing.

# Five - New York City

**Map 3. New York City Lighthouses**

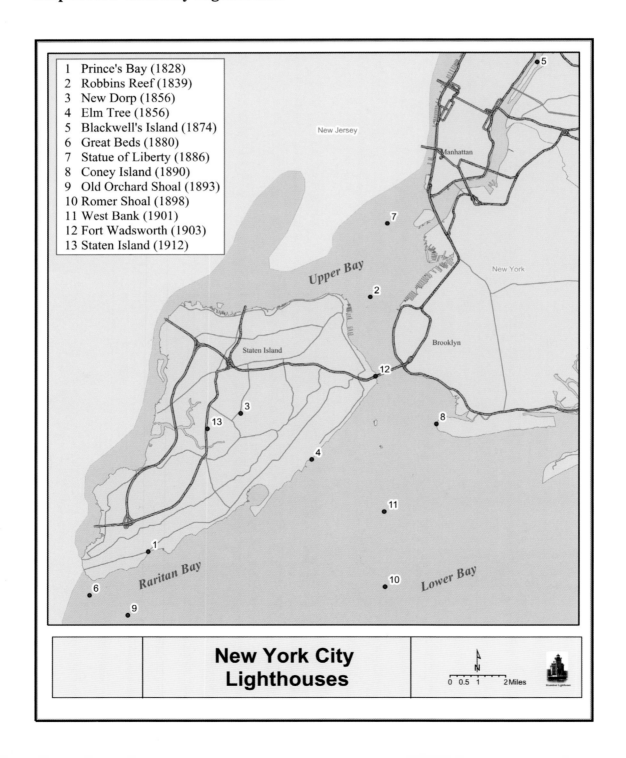

1 Prince's Bay (1828)
2 Robbins Reef (1839)
3 New Dorp (1856)
4 Elm Tree (1856)
5 Blackwell's Island (1874)
6 Great Beds (1880)
7 Statue of Liberty (1886)
8 Coney Island (1890)
9 Old Orchard Shoal (1893)
10 Romer Shoal (1898)
11 West Bank (1901)
12 Fort Wadsworth (1903)
13 Staten Island (1912)

New Jersey

Manhattan

New York

Upper Bay

Brooklyn

Staten Island

Raritan Bay

Lower Bay

**New York City Lighthouses**

N

0  0.5  1        2 Miles

# New York City and the Harbor

Until 1737 there was not one aid to navigation at the entrance to the New York City Harbor from the ocean. In order to protect investments of cargo entering the harbor, the New York State Assembly sponsored a lottery to build the Sandy Hook Lighthouse. Although officially not in New York State, Sandy Hook is often considered one of the New York Harbor lighthouses. The oldest standing active lighthouse in America, was constructed in 1764. It was replaced in 1769 by a brick and stone tower and is still a vital part of New York State maritime history.

New York businessmen also recognized the importance of navigation aids. The first lighthouse constructed in New York City was the Princess Bay Light in 1828. As New York expanded and became the major port in America, bypassing Philadelphia, a need for more lighthouses grew.

Travel to and from New York Harbor begins at a sand bar, seven miles east of Sandy Hook, 25 miles from Manhattan. The entrance to New York Harbor required a captain to travel towards Sandy Hook to the southwest before entering in the main ship channel. It wasn't until 1907 that the U.S. Government dug a channel, 2,000 feet wide by 40 feet deep across the elbow, to save over three miles of travel between New York City and the ocean. It was later deepened to its current depth of 45 feet. This channel was named after Dr. John Wolfe Ambrose, a physician and engineer, who battled Congress for an appropriation for the construction of the channel. Dr. Ambrose died before he realized his dream of a shorter passage to Manhattan.

Additional waterways in the New York City area include the Raritan Bay, Arthur Kill, Kill Van Kull around Staten Island, and the East River around Manhattan Island. In the East River there are six main islands: Governors, Roosevelt, Wards, Randalls, Brother, and North Brother. Many lighthouses were constructed at the outer harbor, near Staten Island and in the East River.

The most difficult area of passage and navigation is Hell's Gate, which is the eastern entrance to the East River from Long Island Sound. Adrian Block was a brave sailor who traveled up the East River past Manhattan Island, around the dangerous rocks and through the currents of Hell's Gate in 1614. During Colonial times there was a story that a murderer was once manacled with chains that been fastened to the rocks at low tide at Hell's Gate.

Half of the disasters came from Pot Rock in Hell's Gate, where the water was only eight feet deep. So in 1850, a lighthouse was constructed on the outcropping rock in Great Neck. Between 1852 and 1918, the U.S. Army Corps of Engineers spent over $6.5 million dollars on the East River project, mostly blasting at Hell's Gate. Today the channel's width has doubled from 600 to 1,200 feet and is 35 feet deep at low tide. Detailed accounts of over 1,000 shipwrecks that occurred between Sandy Hook and Execution Rocks from 1614 to 1972 are contained in *The Perils of the Port of New York* by Jeannette Edwards Rattray.

# Prince's Bay (1828, 1864)

In 1826 a $30,000 appropriation was made for the first lighthouse located near the eastern shoreline's highest point on Staten Island. Constructed and established in 1828, the tower light was built from ruble stone and displayed a fixed white light at an elevation of 106 feet above sea level. In 1837, the Navy recommended that the station could better serve coastal travelers, or coasters, bound from New Jersey to New York, by placing additional reflectors to the west. In 1864, a new brownstone tower was built and in 1868, a Gothic style keeper's house was erected. The keeper's quarter's first floor had a kitchen, pantry, dining room, and sitting room. The second floor had four rooms and an attic.

The new tower was fitted with Three and One-half Order lens in 1857 that displayed varied flashing light. In 1890, the lens was replaced with a Fourth-Order lens with a light that flashed every five seconds. Inside the tower was a cast-iron staircase, which wound around a central pillar. The lens was operated by weight-activated clockworks, which had to be wound every four hours. After acetylene lights were constructed along Raritan Bay in 1822, the Prince's Bay Light was no longer needed and was extinguished.

The Mission of the Immaculate Virgin surrounded the lighthouse property on the north, west, and south. The Mission was a residence and school for 1,400 orphans. After a public auction in 1926, the Mission successfully acquired the eight-acre parcel from the government. The lantern room atop the lighthouse was replaced with a statue of the Blessed Virgin Mary when the Mission bought the property. The statue was lit at night and could be seen from Hylan Boulevard, Staten Island. Until 1988 the keeper's house was used by the Archdiocese of New York as a residence and retreat house for Cardinal John J. O'Conner.

Today, the property is part of the Mount Loretto Unique Area, which is an open space park in Staten Island, operated by New York State Department of Environmental Conservation. The statue of the Blessed Virgin Mary was removed when the State of New York operated the property and turned it into a residence for the park ranger. The Mount Loretto Unique Area is located off Hylan Boulevard in Staten Island in Prince's Bay.

Prince's Bay – Now owned by the New York State Department of Environmental Conservation, it was originally owned by the Archdiocese of New York. Today there is parking on Hylan Boulevard and the grounds surrounding the light are open to the public.

## Range Lights

Sometimes lights in channels or rivers were constructed in pairs as aids to navigation. These pairs are called range lights. The range lights help aid mariners in busy waters. At the New York City Harbor entrance two sets of range lights were constructed to assist navigation, one pair for the Swash Channel and one pair for the Ambrose Channel.

The pairs for the Swash Channel were the Elm Tree and New Dorp Lights. The pairs for the Ambrose Channel were the West Bank and Staten Island Lighthouses. One of the two lights was designated as the front range and the other as the rear range. The New Dorp was rear range and the Elm Tree Lighthouse was the Front Range light. Similarly the Staten Island Lighthouse was the rear range and West Bank was the front range. Ship captains can identify exact coordinates by aligning their vessels with the two range lights.

# Robins Reef (1839, 1883)

Robbins Reef, two miles southwest of the Statue of Liberty, can be seen from the Staten Island Ferry. The current brown and white cast-iron tower, which resembles a spark plug, was constructed in 1883 a few yards south of original light's foundation. Established in 1839, the tower is 56 feet above sea level and had a Fourth-Order lens with a flashing white light. In 1939 the lamp was upgraded with an incandescent oil vapor lamp with 24,000-candlepower, along with an electric-diaphragm foghorn.

Robbins Reef has a rich history of keepers. The first was Jacob Walker, the assistant keeper of the Sandy Hook Lighthouse. In 1882, he met and fell in love with Katherine (Katie) Gortler, who was a young German immigrant. They got married and Katie gave birth to the first of their two children. In December 1885, Jacob was transferred to the Robbins Reef Light as keeper. Katie found the move to the island quite a contrast to Sandy Hook where she had chickens, a garden, and wonderful beaches to walk on. The accommodations at Robbins Reef consisted of a couple of rooms and provided no opportunities to recreate, garden, or view lower Manhattan.

During the winter of 1890, Jacob caught a cold that progressed to pneumonia and was hospitalized at the Smith Infirmary on Staten Island. Although Katie wanted to be with her husband Jacob, she remained at the station to fulfill her husband's responsibilities as head keeper. Sadly, in February 1890 Jacob succumbed to the illness.

The Lighthouse Board offered the position to two different men but both declined the offer. Katie, who remained at the lighthouse, was appointed as keeper with her two children. During her tenure as keeper, Katie raised her two children, tended the light, and saved as many as 50 lives. She was keeper at the light for 29 years until 1919. She lived to the age of 84 and died in 1930. The Coast Guard recognized her achievement by naming a buoy tender ship after her. More can be learned about Katie and her female counterparts of the Lighthouse Service in *Women Who Kept the Lights* by Mary Louise and J. Candice Clifford.

When the Coast Guard took over the Lighthouse Service in 1939, four men were assigned to the station. Three men remained at the Reef while the fourth rotated ashore for five days of leave. In 1965 the station personnel were removed and the station was run remotely with a cable from the Coast Guard Station at St. George, Staten Island. The best way to view the lighthouse is from the Staten Island Ferry.

Robbins Reef – This light is two miles southwest of the Statue of Liberty and can be viewed from the Staten Island Ferry. Katie Walker was the keeper for 29 years and saved over 50 lives at Robbins Reef.

# New Dorp (1856)

The New Dorp light was established in 1856 and the first keeper was John Fountain. The first illuminating apparatus was a Second-Order lens with a fixed red light. The lighthouse is 40 feet high and is 192 feet above sea level. In 1891, the light was changed to fixed white and in 1939 the lens was changed to a Sixth-Order Lens with a fixed white light.

In 1964 the New Dorp light was extinguished and the building was boarded up. Ten years later, the property was auctioned and a young engineer, John Vokral, bought the property for $32,000. Because the property had been heavily vandalized Mr. Vokral had to rebuild the entire structure. Every inch of exterior clapboard needed to be sanded and painted. The wooden floors were refinished, but not until after all 1,286 pegs were hammered and set. It is now a private residence located at the top of Altamont Street in Staten Island. It has been dedicated as New York City landmark.

New Dorp – Although only 40-feet tall, the New Dorp Light is 192 feet above sea level. Because of its location on Staten Island, New Dorp and Elm Tree were paired as range lights. This light was extinguished in 1964 and is now a private residence.

# Elm Tree (1856, 1939)

Richard Calrow constructed both the Elm Tree and the New Dorp as the front and rear range lights. These two lights were used as points of reference for mariners in the Swash Channel. The first illuminating apparatus for the 60-foot Elm Tree Light was a Third-Order lens with a fixed white light. In the 1920s, it was within the perimeter of Miller Field (airfield), at the south shore of Staten Island.

In 1939, the wooden tower was torn down, and a 65-foot concrete tower was erected and also functioned as an aviation tower for Miller Field. After 1939, the tower was maintained by New York City. It flashed alternating green and white lights, helped both aircraft and ships, and was extinguished in 1964.

Elm Tree – Located near Miller Air Field, the concrete tower once functioned as a lighthouse and a guide for aircraft. The Elm Tree Light was named by Dutch sailors who used old Elm trees on Staten Island as landmarks for navigation.

# Blackwell's Island (1874)

The Blackwell's Island lighthouse is visible to motorists along the Franklin D. Roosevelt (FDR) Drive, along the East River in Manhattan. The light marks the entrance to Hell's Gate and a rock reef on the eastern end of Roosevelt Island, called "Bread and Cheese." Blackwell's Island is a slender stone lighthouse which extends to a height of 42 feet. During low tide, the water at this reef is only seven feet deep. The outgoing tide, or ebb tide, often carried unsuspecting vessels onto the dangerous shallow rock reef.

This lighthouse was named after the Blackwell family who owned the island from 1685 to 1823. Constructed in 1874, the lighthouse was designed by James Renwick, the same architect who designed St. Patrick's Cathedral. It was built and maintained by New York City and contained a Fourth-Order lens with fixed red light. In 1874 the light was converted to a gas lamp. By 1975 Roosevelt Island was established as a residential community, having spectacular views of the Manhattan skyline.

Today the light no longer operates as an aid to navigation, but the New York City Department of Parks and Recreation maintains the grounds as Lighthouse Park. The lighthouse can be viewed from Carl Shurz Park off FDR Drive from the west or Hallets Cove from the east. The lighthouse was placed on National Historic Registry of Historic Sites in 1976.

Blackwell's Island – This Gothic-style light was built from gray gneiss and granite found on Roosevelt Island.

# Great Beds (1880)

Ship captains often complained of a shoal near Ward's Point, Staten Island in Raritan Bay. After a petition to the Light House Establishment in 1868, Congress appropriated $34,000 in 1878 to locate this lighthouse at the extreme end of Great Beds Shoal. Great Beds is a tapered steel tower that rises 60 feet above the bay. Cast-iron caisson construction is similar to Robbins Reef and Roamer Shoal.

David Johnson was appointed as the first keeper at Great Beds. When the Civil War broke out in April 1861, Johnson joined the Pennsylvania Calvary and served as a scout and wagon master. Johnson also served in some capacity at the Shinnecock and Montauk Point Lighthouses. The Coast Guard automated the lighthouse in 1945 and to this day, there is controversy as to whether the light is located in New York or New Jersey. The best views of the lighthouse can be seen from Conference Park Beach in Staten Island, New York or in Perth Amboy, New Jersey along the Harbor Walk.

Great Beds –
The 60-foot cast-iron caisson light is similar to Robbin's Reef and Roamer Shoal Lights.

# Statue of Liberty (1886)

A gift from France on July 4, 1884, Lady Liberty was a magnificent creation by artist Frederic Auguste Bartholdi. As a symbol of freedom in America, the Statue Liberty has touched the lives, hearts, and souls of many millions of Americans whose ancestry entered through neighboring Ellis Island.

Gustave Eiffel, who would later design one of Paris's signature landmarks, assisted Bartholdi with the design of the steel frame. Attached to the frame are more than 300 copper plates, between 1/8 and 1/10 of inch thick, and took nearly six years to build in a Paris courtyard. The copper sheets were pounded into many elaborate molds, a technique known as repousee. It was said that the face of Lady Liberty resembled Bartholdi's mother. It took 214 crates to ship it here.

Originally lit on October 28, 1886, the Statue of Liberty was designated a National Monument on October 15, 1924. The statue is positioned on a stone base that stands over 300 feet in New York Harbor, visible to millions of travelers by land, sea, and air. The statue cost $250,000 while the base cost $280,000.

President Grover Cleveland instructed the Secretary of the Treasury to place the Statue of Liberty under the care of the Lighthouse Service. A dynamo to produce electricity was constructed on Bedloe Island, which powered nine arc lamps in the Statue's torch. The lit torch can be recognized as far as 24 miles outside New York Harbor. The Light House Service struggled with their responsibility of maintaining the State of Liberty. The War Department asked the Light House Service to relinquish its jurisdiction over the Statue in November 1901. On March 2, 1902, the Statue was discontinued as aid to navigation. In 1924 President Calvin Coolidge renamed Bedloe's Island to Liberty Island.

In 1986, a French-American Centennial committee was formed to restore the Statue of Liberty. The committee was headed by the former Chairman of Chrysler Corporation, Lee Iacocca. Over $295 million was collected, mostly from the American people. Seventy million was used for the restoration of the Statue; the balance was used for refurbishing Liberty Island. To start the reconditioning task, the world's largest freestanding scaffold was erected, rising 300 feet around the statue and pedestal. The torch was removed because it was beyond repair, and the old torch served as a model for the new one. The reconditioned torch was replaced with 24-karat gold leaf plates, to give the appearance of a bright flame.

All 1,825 support bars that made up the statue's rib work had to be replaced. Additionally, 325 flat bars, 2,000 saddles, and 12,000 rivets were replaced. Seven layers of lead-based paint were removed by using a pressurized liquid nitrogen spray system. After the paint was removed, two layers of tar were blasted using 40 tons of baking soda.

In 1986, Liberty Weekend was a grand celebration for the American and French people. Several days of ceremonies were planned, beginning with an opening ceremony on Governors Island, headed by President Reagan and French President Francois Mitterrand. During that evening on Ellis Island, Chief Justice Earl Warren Burger, with the aid of satellite communication, naturalized 27,000 new Americans. On Friday July 4, 30,000 vessels from kayaks to the ocean liner, Queen Elizabeth II, dotted New York Harbor. Six million people converged upon lower Manhattan, Staten Island, Brooklyn, and New Jersey. Cruising down the Hudson River, the USS Battleship Iowa fired a twenty-one-gun salute with President Reagan aboard. Twenty-two tall ships from 18 countries also graced New York Harbor in a parade of nations that was televised across the world. By dusk, 32 barges were strategically placed for the largest pyrotechnic displays ever viewed. The fireworks, also called the Big Bang, lasted 28 minutes and consisted of 400,000 projectiles.

The party continued on the actual 100th anniversary of the statue's dedication. On October 28, 1986, a ticker-tape parade along Broadway included 2.2 million spectators. A smaller ceremony with 1,500 people took place on Liberty Island later that day. During that ceremony, the Statue of Liberty was inducted as one of the 80 World Heritage Sites, joining such notables as the Palace of Versailles and the Pyramids.

Climbing 168-step spiral staircase to the crown of the Statue reveals an incredible view of the New York Harbor. Visitors from around the world can visit the Statue of Liberty every day except for Christmas. The National Park Service manages the 12-acre island; ferry service to the island leaves Battery Park in lower Manhattan and Liberty State Park in New Jersey. Although not regarded today as an aid to navigation, the Statue has a light in the torch area, which shines through many glass windows.

Statue of Liberty – Lady Liberty photographed in July 2001, just two months prior to the tragic act of terrorism on the World Trade Center.

Statue of Liberty – In 1886, the Statue of Liberty was the first lighthouse in America to be electrified.

# Coney Island (1890)

The Coney Island Lighthouse was established in 1890 and is located at the far western part of Brooklyn's shore, known as Norton's Point. The 75-foot white steel tower flashes red and is still an aid to navigation. The Coney Island Lighthouse was a copy of the Throg's Neck Lighthouse. The Coney Island Lighthouse was originally constructed as a rear range light. The front range light, a square skeleton tower, was erected between B47 and B48 Streets in the community of Sea Gate. The original Fourth-Order lens was removed in 1989 and briefly displayed at the South Street Seaport. Today mariners can view the modern red beacon through a 190-mm Fresnel lens with a 1000-watt lamp that flashes every five seconds.

Thomas Higginbotham was the first keeper who served till 1908; he was followed by Herbert Greenwood (1908-1944) and Adrian Boisvert (1944-1960). Frank Schubert served as keeper of the Coney Island Lighthouse until his death in 2003. Schubert had a long and interesting life working as a public servant, working a variety of marine-related careers. He started in the Coast Guard and in 1937 was appointed seaman on the Lighthouse Tender, the *Tulip*. A lighthouse tender is a ship specifically designed to maintain, support, or tend to lighthouses providing supplies, fuel, mail and transportation. In the United States, these ships originally served as part of the Lighthouse Service and are now are part of the Coast Guard.

After serving on the *Tulip* and assisting in New York Harbor for 2.5 years, Schubert was appointed keeper at Old Orchard Lighthouse until 1942. He was then assigned to Governor's Island Light, when he was drafted by the Navy. He was assigned to Camp Gordon Johnson in Florida to be a naval landing craft instructor. After he was dismissed from the Navy in 1944, Schubert was reassigned to Governor's Island. In July 1960, he was appointed keeper at Coney Island Light where he served and lived with his wife Millie and three children. The Coney Island Light was automated in 1989, but Mr. Schubert was allowed to remain at the light to maintain the dwellings. Mr. Schubert was invited to meet with President George Bush Sr. at the White House. The lighthouse is located in Sea Gate, a private community off 46th Street in Brooklyn.

Coney Island – Located at Norton Point in the community of Sea Gate, a red beacon flashes every five seconds. Frank Schubert, who served at Coney Island, was the last civilian light keeper in the country. He served from 1960 until 2003.

# Old Orchard Shoal (1893)

There was great increase in shipping traffic through Prince's Bay in the late 1800s because of the railroad bridges built across Staten Island Sound from New Jersey. Many barges were moved by tugs in the narrow waterway near Old Orchard and West Bank Shoals. In 1891, the Light House Service requested an appropriation of $60,000 from Congress for a light at Old Orchard and Waackaack. The Old Orchard Light was established on April 25, 1893, along with the Waackaack Beacon as a front range light for the Gedney Channel. The station was equipped with a Fourth-Order Fresnel lens with an eclipsed white lamp. Alfred Calrow, the station's first keeper, had previously served on the Sandy Hook and Scotland Lightships.

Old Orchard Light stands three miles off Staten Island. Confinement and boredom often affected keepers of this isolated station. In September 1902, Keeper Calrow was hospitalized for nervous exhaustion at the Marine Hospital in New York and was relieved of his duty. He never returned to work for the Lighthouse Service.

Andrew Zuius, the second keeper, performed many rescues at Old Orchard. During a storm in June 1927, Zuius rescued four men whose motorboat had sunk. Often after the rescue, the victims needed shelter, dry clothing, and warm meal which meant the light station became accommodations for unexpected guests.

The Waackaack Beacon has been removed, so the Old Orchard no longer functions as range light. The Coast Guard automated the light in 1955 and it flashes a white light with a red sector to warn boaters of the dangerous shoal off Staten Island. Old Orchard is best viewed from the water in Staten Island or Perth Amboy, New Jersey.

Old Orchard Shoal – Photographed three weeks after September 11, 2001; only sailing ships in competition were permitted to travel freely in the New York Harbor.

Old Orchard Shoal – This light is located three miles off Staten Island. This 35-foot tower is still an active aid-to-navigation.

# Romer Shoal (1898)

Before the Romer Shoal Light was built, a day marker was established in 1838 to warn shipping captains. In 1886, a 25-foot skeleton tower, which had a 90-day supply of compressed gas, was first lit. The tower required a great deal of maintenance. It broke down and needed repairs frequently, which prompted the decision to erect a lighthouse in its place. Construction of the lighthouse began in May 1898 and was completed by October. The first lighting apparatus was a Fifth-Order Fresnel lens with a fixed red lamp at an elevation of 54 feet. The cast-iron conical tower had accommodations for three keepers.

The Great Northeast Hurricane of September 1938 caused many deaths and much destruction in Long Island and Connecticut. At Romer Shoal, moderate winds began in the morning and shifted to strong northerly gale-force winds. Keeper Herman Westgate noted in the keepers log that the barometric pressure had fallen to 28.72 inches and the water near the shoal had turned black. The Romer Shoal sustained extensive damage from the hurricane while other lighthouses further up the coast escaped relatively unscathed.

During the First World War, the Navy stationed personnel in the lighthouse to keep track of vessels entering and leaving the harbor. The United States Coast Guard took over the duties of the light in 1939 and automated it in 1966. Romer Shoal remained on the Lighthouse Doomsday list until it was recently reinstated as an active navigational aid.

Romer Shoal can best be viewed by boat, at the far lower bay, several miles from New York City and Staten Island in Swash Channel.

Romer Shoal – This light was used as a training lighthouse for the Lighthouse Depot on Staten Island. The Depot served as a warehouse and repair shop for lighthouses nearby. The lighthouse was named after the pilot boat, William Roamer, which sank near the site in 1863.

# West Bank (1901)

Located 4.7 miles south of the Verrazano-Narrows Bridge, West Bank was constructed as part of the improvements to New York City Harbor, which included the dredging of Ambrose Channel. A conical, spark plug-shaped tower was built on a steel caisson, which was floated in place, sunk, and filled with concrete. On top of the caisson foundation was the tower's 135,000-pound superstructure. Construction was completed by January 1, 1901 and a Fourth-Order lens with a fixed white light with red reflector was lit.

The West Bank Lighthouse was built to be the front range light with the Staten Island Light as the rear range light. In 1906, Congress appropriated funds for the lighting of Ambrose Channel. This included the Ambrose Lightship, North Hook Beacon, and raising the height of the West Bank Lighthouse. Two additional stories were added to the West Bank's tower, raising the beacon height to 70 feet. This made it the tallest of all New York offshore lights.

Otto Banks, the last civilian keeper, served at West Bank until 1956. The Coast Guard automated the light in 1985. West Bank was the last of the lighthouses in the Third District to be staffed by Coast Guard personnel. The Fourth-Order lens was removed and replaced with new modern optic, which has a fixed white light with a red sector. Solar panels assist with the operation of the light by recharging the beacon's storage batteries. Today the light remains an aid to navigation for the many shipping vessels entering and leaving New York Harbor. West Bank can best be viewed by boat several miles from New York City.

West Bank – West Bank was constructed in 1901 to assist with the navigation in the Ambrose Channel that was a more direct route to New York City Harbor. The West Bank Light was automated in 1985 and flashes a fixed white light with a red sector.

# Fort Wadsworth (1903)

When a ship entered New York Harbor, navigation through the narrows was treacherous. This difficult path was first encountered by Giovanni Da Verrazano in 1524. In 1828, Fort Tompkins Light was built and in 1873, Fort Tompkins lighthouse was rebuilt. The first light needed to be relocated because it was damaged during artillery practice. The second location was ineffective because it was too far back from the point. Then a lighthouse and fog signal was proposed for Fort Wadsworth. A fog signal was established at Fort Lafayette in 1873, which assisted vessels bound to and from Coney Island, but it was not useful for those traveling through the Narrows.

In October 1902, construction began on a new 75-foot tower at Fort Wadsworth and was completed on March 1, 1903. The black lighthouse lantern room contained a Fourth-Order lens with a flashing white and red light that was visible for 14 miles. The first keeper was William Boyle when the lighthouse was established. In 1941 the lamps were changed to green and white flashing light to accommodate both aviators (green) and mariners (white).

It was an active aid to navigation until 1965, when the building of the Verrazano-Narrows Bridge rendered it obsolete. In 1995, the Fort Wadsworth property was transferred to the National Park Service as part of the Gateway Recreational Area. In 2002, the National Park Service volunteers, led by Joe Esposito, developed a plan for saving Fort Wadsworth Lighthouse and convinced the National Park Service to restore the light. On September 24, 2005, a new $27,000 solar-powered system was lit, almost 40 years after the light had been extinguished. It is located at the west end of the Verrazano-Narrows Bridge and can be viewed from a bluff at the eastern end of the Fort and is part of the National Park Service Gateway Recreational Area.

Fort Wadsworth – This photograph was taken prior ot September 2005, when a new solar-powered system was lit.

Fort Wadsworth – The new Fort Wadsworth was built to replace Fort Tompkins and is located at the narrows of New York City next to the Verrazano Bridge.

# Staten Island (1912)

Constructed at 231 feet above sea level, the Staten Island Light is an octagonal, light-colored, brick tower. The 90-foot tower is built on a gray limestone foundation and was built as the rear range light for West Bank Light. Established on April 15, 1912, the lighthouse contained a Second-Order bivalve lens with a 1500-candlepower kerosene vapor lamp. The Second-Order Fresnel lens improved the efficiency of the lamp by 200 times. The keeper's dwelling, constructed of the same materials as the tower, is 150 feet east of the lighthouse.

Today it has been automated with a modern 18-mm lens with a range of 5.5 miles. The lighthouse seems out of place because it is in the heart of Richmond Hill, a quaint residential community in Staten Island. The lighthouse is located at Richmond Road and Lighthouse Avenue, near La Tourette Park. The keeper's dwelling is a private residence and the beacon is not open to the public. In 1968, it was designated a New York City Historic Landmark.

Staten Island – The 90-foot octagonal brick Staten Island Light sits at an elevation of 231 feet above sea level in what now is a residential neighborhood.

Staten Island – This light was built as a rear range light along with the offshore West Bank that functioned as the front range light.

# Six - Hudson River Valley

**Map 4. Hudson River Lighthouses**

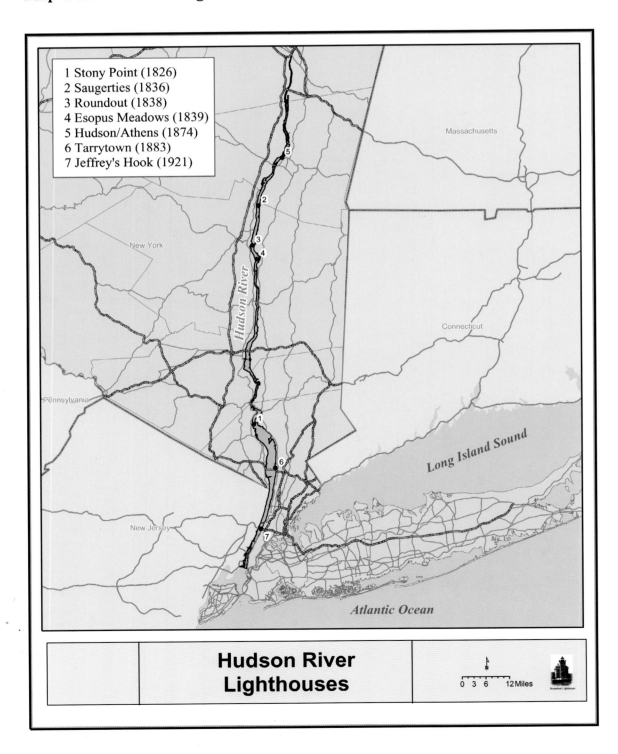

1 Stony Point (1826)
2 Saugerties (1836)
3 Roundout (1838)
4 Esopus Meadows (1839)
5 Hudson/Athens (1874)
6 Tarrytown (1883)
7 Jeffrey's Hook (1921)

Massachusetts

New York

Hudson River

Connecticut

Pennsylvania

Long Island Sound

New Jersey

Atlantic Ocean

**Hudson River Lighthouses**

0 3 6 12 Miles

# Hudson River

The famous Hudson River starts at Lake Tear of the Clouds, at the shoulder of Mt. Marcy in the Adirondacks, the highest point in New York (5,344 feet). The water flows 315 miles before reaching the southern tip of Manhattan at the Battery. Although not the largest estuary in America, the Hudson River Basin includes eastern and northern New York, Vermont, Massachusetts, Connecticut, and New Jersey, a total of 13,390 square miles. The river is 3.5 miles wide at the Tappan Zee Bridge, which connects Nyack and Tarrytown. The river's elevation has a four to five foot rise during the tidal flow up to the Troy dam, which is 153 miles north of the Battery. The river is 216 feet deep at Matry's Reach, near West Point.

## Discovery and Colonization

The Hudson Valley has a rich history filled with tales of trading and colonization. The American Revolution, the industrialization of America with the Erie and Champlain Canals, and the well-known writers and artists of the Hudson River School, are all characteristic of the Hudson Valley.

On September 12, 1609, Henry Hudson arrived in Albany in his sailing ship, the *Half Moen*. Although Hudson returned to Europe without finding a passage to the East, Johannes De Laet, director of the Dutch West India Company, documented his impressions of the river in his notes "New World." Because of the rich descriptions captured in this document, other traders from Europe were attracted to America to sail the Hudson River. Two traders lured to New York, or New Netherlands, were Adrian Block and Hendrick Christiansen.

The Dutch set up communities in Manhattan and Fort Orange, which is now Albany, New York's capital city. The Dutch recognized the value of the beaver pelts and established farms adjacent to river in New Amsterdam, Beverwyck, and Esopus. They grew corn, peas, oat and wheat. Because the Dutch also had a taste for beer, they cultivated hops. The vast resources of the Hudson Valley prompted many battles including the American Revolution. Settlers fought over the right to control the land and resources of New Netherlands, which would later be called New York.

## Fulton and the Erie Canal

On August 17, 1807, Robert Fulton sailed the *Clermont*, his first commercial steamship, up the Hudson River. Powered by a single Watt steam engine, the *Clermont* created quite a stir as Fulton navigated to Albany in 34 hours and returned to New York City in thirty hours. The following year, he added two more steamships to the Hudson. By 1811, he added the *New Orleans* to the Mississippi River. By 1851, more than a million passengers were riding in style on the Hudson, Mississippi, and Missouri Rivers.

With the support of Governor Dewitt Clinton, construction of the Erie Canal began in Rome, New York, on July 4, 1817. The 363 mile-long canal with 83 locks, 18 aqueducts, and almost 300 bridges cost the state $7,143,789. The Erie Canal was officially opened on October 26, 1825. Between 1817 and 1836, nine lateral canals were built to connect the northern and southern parts of the state to the Erie Canal. Between 1835 and 1862, the canal was enlarged for a total cost of $30 million dollars. The canal reduced travel time from six weeks to six days and cut the freight costs from $95 to $125 per ton to $4 to $6 per ton. The importance of the canal began to fade as railroads were introduced in the 1850s.

# The Arts and the Hudson Valley

The natural beauty of the Hudson River continues to inspire many artists. The romance of the river was best portrayed by Thomas Cole, who founded the Hudson River School for artist and writers in the 1820s. Asher Durand later joined Cole in using large canvas with exquisite detail to depict the beauty of the majestic Hudson Valley. Cole and Durand mentored John Kensett, Sanford Gifford, and Frederick Church, a second and third generation of painters.

Paralleling these artists were some of the great American writers such as Washington Irving, James Fenimore Cooper, and Herman Melville. The Hudson has been designated as one of America's great rivers and is part of the American Heritage Rivers Initiative.

## Stony Point (1826)

Located on the west bank of the Hudson River below West Point, Stony Point Lighthouse is the oldest light on the Hudson River and was the last one manned. Stony Point was completed in 1826, just one year after the Erie Canal was opened. The 24-foot octagonal tower was constructed on a bluff from blue split stone. By 1895, there were 48 aids to navigation on the Hudson River from Jeffrey's Hook north to Troy. Twelve were lighthouses and the rest were post lamps or towers.

This brightly colored lighthouse is part of the 87-acre Stony Point National Battlefield, owned by the Palisades Park Commission and the New York State Office of Parks, Recreation and Historic Preservation. Nancy Rose, a brave lighthouse keeper for more than 40 years, lived there from 1859 to 1904. The tower was refurbished and the new keeper's quarter was built in 1879. There were eight women and men who were keepers at this light.

Stony Point Light Station was decommissioned in 1925 and automated by the Coast Guard in 1973. It was restored in 1986 and the lamp was relit on October 7, 1995, with a Fourth-Order Fresnel lens, flashing every four seconds.

Stony Point – This is the oldest lighthouse on the Hudson River, established in 1826, just after the opening of the Erie Canal in 1825. Located on a high bluff, the 24-foot tower sits at 178 feet above sea level and can be seen for 22 miles.

The Stony Point Lighthouse is located on a high peninsula which juts out into the Hudson at Haverstraw Bay. From the lighthouse vantage point, visitors can see the Tappan Zee Bridge to the south. To the north is Jones Point and South Gate, which are part of the Appalachian Mountains.

Stony Point is open to the public whenever the Stony Point Battlefield State Historic Site is in operation. Tours of the lighthouse are available on a regular basis on weekends. The lighthouse is located off Route 9W, north of Stony Point along Park Road.

# Saugerties (1836, 1869)

The Saugerties Lighthouse began construction in 1835 and was completed in 1836 on a 40 foot by 50 foot rock-filled crib pier. Located on the north bank of Esopus Creek, at the confluence of the Hudson River, the station's light was upgraded to a Sixth-Order lens in 1854. In 1966, the Hudson Valley River Commission intervened when the Coast Guard wanted to demolish the Saugerties and Esopus Meadows Lights. Saugerties was placed on the National Register of Historic Places in 1974. In 1987, it was purchased by the Saugerties Lighthouse Conservancy for one dollar from New York State, and was refurbished and relit on August 4, 1990, by the Conservancy.

Today, it can be enjoyed as a Bed and Breakfast. The lighthouse contains a small museum, gift shop, parlor, kitchen, keeper's quarters and two guest bedrooms. Saugerties is accessible by boat or via the half-mile nature trail through the Ruth R. Glunt Nature Preserve, a 17-acre tidal river wetland area off Lighthouse Drive. Visitors are welcome during the day to visit the grounds of the lighthouse.

Saugerties – During low tide, the mud flats provide easy access to the lighthouse. Many bring their pets or fishing poles to recreate at the lighthouse.

Saugerties – Saugerties Lighthouse Conservancy purchased the lighthouse for one dollar. They refurbished the structure and now operate a bed and breakfast, which has two guest rooms.

# Rondout (1838, 1867, 1915)

The current Rondout Lighthouse is actually the third lighthouse built at the mouth of Rondout Creek. The first Kingston lighthouse was built in 1838. The wood structure was badly damaged by ice and weather and became unsafe for the keeper and his family. A second lighthouse was constructed of brick and stone in 1867 on the south side of the creek. It was abandoned in 1915 and demolished in 1954; today all that remains are the stone footings. The largest and last family lighthouse built on the Hudson was established here on August 25, 1915.

George Murdock became keeper of the Rondout Lighthouse in 1856. George, who had married Catherine Parsell from Esopus, died tragically only one year after his appointment in a drowning accident. His wife, Catherine, was appointed keeper and remained there with her children until 1907. She lived a rich life on the river raising her children, telling stories about steamboat races and the many rescues she made. Their son, James, tended the light from 1907 to 1922. In total, the Murdock family served for 67 years.

The Rondout Lighthouse was a family-occupied lighthouse until 1946 when the Coast Guard took over. Electricity was installed in 1946 and in 1954 the lighthouse was boarded up. Today the Rondout is open for public tours, conducted by the Mid-Hudson Estuarine Services.

Rondout – The largest family lighthouse on the Hudson River was constructed in 1915. The Hudson River Maritime Museum, with the help of the city of Kingston, renovated the light and converted it to a museum which is open on weekends in the summer.

# Esopus Meadows (1839, 1872)

The Esopus Meadows Lighthouse was lit for the first time in 1839. However, by 1867, the site was described as being "in ruinous condition" and the pier for the lighthouse was at risk by ice and spring flooding. The current Esopus Meadows Lighthouse was completed in 1872. The foundation for the light consists of 250, forty-foot long wooden piles, driven into the riverbed. A round granite-faced pier, 49 feet in diameter, contains a keeper's dwelling with a lantern room which 52 feet above sea level. Esopus Meadows has a spectacular view of the Catskill Mountains and is the only remaining wooden lighthouse on the Hudson River.

It was placed on the National Register of Historical Places in 1979. In 1990, the Save the Esopus Meadows Lighthouse Commission was created to restore this deteriorating structure. The U.S. Coast Guard leased the lighthouse to the group until September 2002. On September 22, 2002, it was officially transferred from the government to the Commission. The Esopus Lighthouse can be viewed by boarding the *Rip Van Winkle* tour boat out of Historic Kingston.

Esopus Meadows – Esopus Meadows is the only wooden lighthouse on the Hudson River and was established in 1839.

Esopus Meadows – The lighthouse is currently under restoration.
The curtains in the lower middle window are painted on wood.

# Hudson-Athens (1874)

Also known as the Hudson City Lighthouse, this is the northern most of the remaining Hudson River lighthouses. Located just south of Middle Ground Flats, this bright red brick lighthouse is 54-feet above sea level. Originally the lighthouse had Sixth-Order lens which was upgraded to Fifth-Order lens in 1939 with a 2,100-candlepower flashing white light. Also a bell-struck fog signal was installed in 1907, which rang every 15 seconds.

Its design is similar to the Stepping Stones Lighthouse in Long Island Sound. The station's first keeper, Henry J. Best, was appointed to the post in September 1874 and was credited with several rescues during his time. In 1912, the keeper removed eleven women from the steamer, *Isabella*, which had collided with a tug near the lighthouse.

Emil J. Brunner served as light keeper from 1932 to 1950 was paid $80 per month. His family lived in the lighthouse until 1937. Mr. Brunner was depicted on the cover of the December 28, 1946, issue of *Saturday Evening Post*, rowing across the Hudson River with his son and a Christmas tree. Coast Guardsman G. E. Speaks was the last keeper of the Hudson-Athens Lighthouse as the lighthouse was automated on November 10, 1949.

In 1984, the Hudson-Athens Lighthouse Preservation Society (HALPS) signed a lease with the Coast Guard to maintain the lighthouse. After many thousands of hours of work, the Coast Guard officially transferred the title over to the Preservation Society in July 2000. It was an exciting day for me, as I witnessed the transfer. As a member HALPS, I have helped the Preservation Society by giving tours of this beautifully restored gothic-style lighthouse.

HALPS has fully restored the exterior and interior of the lighthouse with furnishings from the 1930s. New exhibits and lighthouse memorabilia can be seen on the tours in the late spring, summer and early fall. The Hudson Light website contains specifics on the schedule. The best vantage point to view and photograph this lighthouse is just south of the Hudson rail station along the eastern shore.

Hudson-Athens – This light is located just south of Middle Ground Flats in the Hudson River and is accessible by boat from the town of Athens or the city of Hudson. The Hudson Athens Lighthouse Preservation Society provides tours during the summer and early fall. Visit their website to find more details.

# Tarrytown (1883)

Within sight of the Tappan Zee Bridge, near the former General Motors Plant in Tarrytown, this cast iron lighthouse tower is 56 feet above sea level. The lighthouse was established on October 1, 1883, and Jacob Ackerman was the first keeper. In 1891, a fog signal was added which rang every 20 seconds. In May 1902, a clockworks mechanism was added, which changed the characteristic of the light to flash red every four seconds.

The assignment of the Tarrytown Light was a good appointment because of its proximity to town. However the challenge was the curved walls and tight quarters that tested the family's creativity during the winter months. The spring and summer months were much more enjoyable for the keeper and his family. Besides tending the light, they enjoyed fishing and watching the wonderful sunsets on the Palisades cliffs.

The importance of the Tarrytown Lighthouse was greatly diminished in 1955 when the Tappan Zee Bridge was built and the beacon became automated in 1959. The light was extinguished in 1961. The County of Westchester acquired the lighthouse in 1974 and the lighthouse was placed on the National Register of Historic Places in 1979. The lighthouse serves as museum for the community and tours are available by appointment. The museum contains artifacts and exhibits that depict the life of a lighthouse keeper and presents the history of the construction of the Tappan Zee Bridge. Tarrytown Lighthouse is located at Kingsland Point Park, a 30-acre county park with picnic facilities, playground and athletic fields.

Tarrytown – Owned by Westchester County, the Tarrytown Light has a marvelous backdrop of the Palisades Cliffs.

Tarrytown – The importance of the Tarrytown Lighthouse was greatly diminished
with the construction of the Tappan Zee Bridge 1955. It was automated in 1959.

# Jeffrey's Hook (1921)

The Jeffrey's Hook Lighthouse is the southern most fixed navigational aid on the Hudson River. From 1870 to 1917, it was located in Sandy Hook, New Jersey. This bright red, conical steel tower was relocated under the George Washington Bridge in 1921. Known as "Little Red," it is the shortest of the Hudson River lighthouses, standing only ten feet high.

The future of the lighthouse was controversial in New York City because its future was threatened by the construction of the bridge. The Coast Guard was to going to auction the light to the highest bidder. A children's book, *The Little Red Lighthouse and Great Gray Bridge* by Hildergarde Swift, was published in 1942 and talked about possibly removing the lighthouse. Subsequently, the Coast Guard was flooded with letters from youngsters expressing their dismay at plans to remove this lighthouse. Because of heightened public awareness, New York City Park's Commissioner, Robert Moses, requested that the lighthouse be transferred to New York City. The lighthouse was extinguished in 1947 and made it available as excess property. It was transferred to the New York City Parks Department in 1951.

In 1982, New York City had the structure repainted and made improvements to the park grounds. Today the Urban Park Rangers conduct educational tours of the lighthouse and hold an annual Little Red Lighthouse Festival. Jeffrey's Hook Lighthouse is located just under the George Washington Bridge at 178th Street and can be reached by taking the Fort Washington exit off Riverside Drive.

Jeffreys Hook – Also known as Little Red, this light was a source of great controversy in New York City when the George Washington Bridge was constructed.

Jeffrey's Hook – The Jeffrey's Hook Light is located in the shadow of the George Washington Bridge, in Fort Washington Park in Manhattan, off Riverside Drive.

# Seven - Lake Champlain

**Map 5. Lake Champlain Lighthouses**

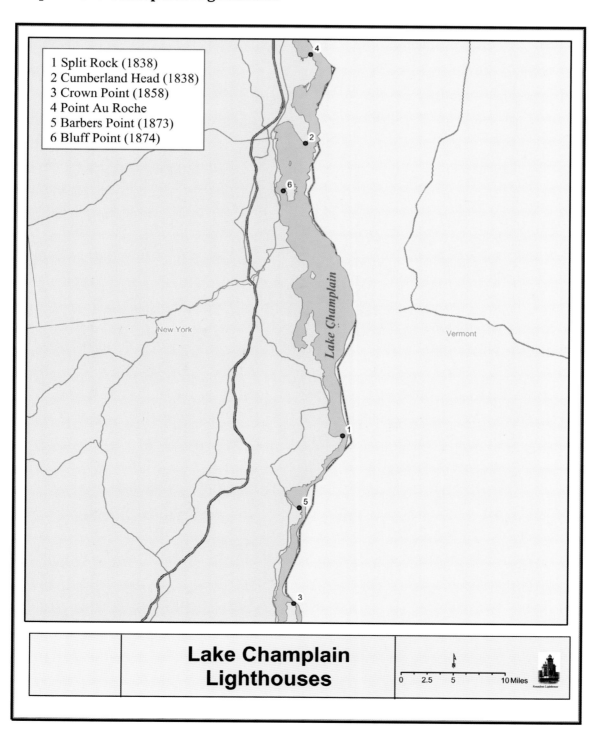

1 Split Rock (1838)
2 Cumberland Head (1838)
3 Crown Point (1858)
4 Point Au Roche
5 Barbers Point (1873)
6 Bluff Point (1874)

Lake Champlain

New York

Vermont

**Lake Champlain
Lighthouses**

0    2.5    5                10 Miles

# Discovery, Battles, World's Second Steamship

On July 3, 1609, Samuel de Champlain first discovered the lake that would be named in his honor. Champlain had been traveling south from the St. Lawrence and then the Richelieu Rivers. This route gave the French settlers that followed Champlain access to many natural resources in addition to passage to France. This area was eventually known as New France.

Lake Champlain contains over 300 shipwrecks. In 1808, the world's second steamship, the *Vermont*, began service just one year after Fulton's famous steamship, the *Clermont*, made its maiden voyage on the Hudson River.

Lake Champlain and the surrounding area were the stage for three wars during the eighteenth and nineteenth centuries. Native Americans had inhabited the area for thousands of years, but as this area was settled and wars broke out, the landscape greatly changed. Opposing armies fought the French and Indian Wars (1755-1760), the Revolutionary War (1775-1783), and the War of 1812 (1812-1814).

Much of this great American history can found by visiting the Lake Champlain Maritime Museum at Basin Harbor in Vergennes, Vermont. The Clinton County Historical Museum in Plattsburgh and the Essex County Museum in Elizabethtown also house interesting Champlain artifacts and history.

## The Lake

Created at the end of the ice age, Lake Champlain shares the same beginning as the Great Lakes. All were carved by the glaciers. Some believe that due to its size and origin, Lake Champlain should be considered one of the Great Lakes. This has been a source of controversy for over 150 years. Looking at size alone, one might question the merit of such a claim, for Lake Champlain's surface area is 6 % of Lake Ontario and only 1.4% of Lake Superior. Lake Champlain is the sixth largest lake in the United States behind Lake Erie. In volume, Lake Erie has a volume of 116 cubic miles, while Lake Champlain contains only 6.1 cubic miles. However, Lake Champlain is 125 miles long, 12 miles wide, has 600 miles of coastline, and is 399 feet at its deepest point. With an average depth of 64 feet, it has a surface area of 435 square miles and a drainage basin of 8,234 square miles. Nevertheless, one may concede that Lake Champlain is truly a great lake, because of its historical and commercial importance.

## The Canal

The Lake Champlain Canal first opened in 1823, just two years before the Erie Canal. It is 63 miles long and consists of 12 locks on the Hudson River that lift vessels 40 feet between Mechanicville and Whitehall, New York. When it first opened, northbound barges returned with manufactured goods such as spirits. Iron ore and lumber. The iron ore processed from the Lake Champlain Basin became the lifeblood flowing through the Canal. This ore was instrumental in the North's success during the Civil War. This same iron ore supplied the iron used for building the railroad that helped settle the West. This canal also facilitated the movement of coffee, coal, and sugar northward.

The Canal expanded four times between 1823 and 1915 to accommodate larger boats and barges. Initially the locks could accommodate cargo boats up to 79 feet; in 1858, this was lengthened to 88 feet. In 1897, the locks were lengthened to 97 feet; in 1915, the locks were rebuilt with concrete and could receive a 300-foot vessel. During the growth along the Canal, the first lighthouse in Lake Champlain was built in 1826 on Juniper Island, Vermont. By end of the nineteenth century, the Lighthouse Board had added nine more lighthouses, ten minor lights, 36 buoys, and 15 post beacons to assist with the navigation through Lake Champlain narrows.

# Split Rock (1838, 1867)

At Split Rock, Lake Champlain is only .75 mile wide and the lake is almost 400-feet deep. Split Rock was also used a boundary for the territory between the Mohawk and Algonquin tribes. In 1832, Congress approved the construction of a lighthouse at Split Rock, making it Lake Champlain's second lighthouse. It was built by Peter Comstick at a cost of $3,225. A Fourth-Order lens with a fix white light was added in 1857. In 1867, the structure was replaced with 39-foot octagonal tower constructed of blue stone. It had a focal plane of 100 feet above the lake, making the light was visible for twelve miles. The keeper's quarters was replaced in 1874.

The Lighthouse Service authorized the construction of a steel skeletal tower to replace the lighthouse in the 1920s. In 1928, a new tower was erected and used acetylene as the light source.

During the Depression, the government decided to surplus the valuable lakefront property and sold it for $2,700 in 1931. The lighthouse, which consists of a Greek revival dwelling and a carriage house, has been well maintained by several private owners. Recently the original light was transferred from the skeleton tower back to the lighthouse tower. On March 19, 2003, after 70 years of darkness, the light beamed again from Split Rock Lighthouse. It sits on private property can be viewed from Lake Champlain, just south of the Essex, Vermont ferry.

Split Rock – Located on a bluff, the 39-foot tower at Split Rock is 100 feet above the lake level. The Greek Revival dwelling and the lighthouse was relit on March 19, 2003, after seventy years of darkness.

# Cumberland Head (1838, 1867)

The Cumberland Head Light was constructed at the point of a very significant battle during the War of 1812. As the British and U.S. Naval fleets fought on September 11, 1814, a decisive victory for Thomas MacDonough was won. MacDonough positioned the American fleet and helped to establish the northern border that soon brought the War of 1812 to an end. The Cumberland Head Light was constructed in 1838 by Peter Comstock, who also built Split Rock Lighthouse.

Cumberland Head was made of native ruble limestone and was illuminated with eleven lamps with reflectors. A Fourth-Order lens with fixed white lamp was installed in 1856. To make the tower more visible to mariners, the tower was disassembled in 1867, and a new 75-foot tower was built and visible for eleven miles. The Victorian-Gothic, two-story keeper's quarters had two large and two small bedrooms, as well as a kitchen, dining-sitting room, parlor, and panty.

William Taberrah, a Civil War veteran, was appointed as keeper of Cumberland Head Light in 1871. When he and his wife moved into the lighthouse, they had two infant children; six more children were born to the Taberrah's during his tenure as keeper. Even though Taberrah had a musket ball lodged in his hip from the war, causing considerable pain, he performed his duties as the keeper for over 33 years. He underwent surgery in 1903 to remove the lead shot from his hip. Several months after the operation, an infection set in and he died. His wife Emma was appointed as keeper on December 19, 1904 and served until 1919 with the assistance of her two daughters.

A steel tower with automated acetylene light was built in 1934 and Cumberland Head was discontinued. In 1946, the land was subdivided and offered at an auction.

In 1948, Joseph Church, a World War II veteran, moved into the abandoned and vandalized structure with his wife. They renovated the keeper's quarters and maintained the lighthouse for the next 50 years until Mrs. Church sold the property in 1996. In March 2003, the Coast Guard helped the new owners to return the light to the tower. Today the Cumberland Head Lighthouse is on the official seal for the Town of Plattsburgh. The light is privately owned and is best viewed from Lake Champlain.

Cumberland Head – The Cumberland Head Light is on the official seal of the Town of Plattsburgh. Today, the 75-foot Cumberland Head stone tower has an automated modern beacon.

# Crown Point (1858)

The Crown Point Lighthouse serves as a beacon and monument to the exploration and navigation of Lake Champlain. The French first erected a windmill in 1737 as part of Fort St. Frederick. Before relinquishing the fort to the British, the French blew up the windmill. The British build a strong defense on Lake Champlain with Fort Crown Point. During the Revolutionary War, "The Green Mountain Boys" took Crown Point and the British regained the fort until the end of the war. Similar in construction to Point Aux Roche and Windmill Point, located at the northern end of the lake, Crown Point Station was established in 1858. The 55-foot octagonal gray limestone block tower was attached to a wooden Cape Cod-style keeper's quarters. The tower sat 83 feet above the lake and contained a Fifth-Order lens, which was visible for eleven miles.

In 1910, Champlain Tercentenary Commission received permission from the newly formed Lighthouse Service to commemorate the discoveries of great explorers by designing a new neoclassical memorial for $50,000. The new design had a base of Fox Island granite, eight Doric columns, an ornate cornice parapet, and a lantern room. Located inside the columns was a cylindrical shaft containing the spiral stairs from the original tower. Samuel de Champlain appears as the central figure in a bronze statue created by Carl Heber. President William H. Taft presided over the dedication in 1912, accompanied by a French government delegation who presented a bronze medallion bust by Augustine Rodin. With the completion of the bridge at Crown Point in 1929, the lighthouse was decommissioned and the keeper's quarters were raised. Today the lighthouse is part of Crown Point State Historic Site and is open year round. Crown Point is a great stopover while traveling to Vermont. There is a state campground here, which is popular for fisherman and boaters.

Crown Point – In 1912, President William H. Taft presided over the dedication of the newly completed Crown Point Light. The light was erected to commemorate the discoveries of Samuel deChamplain.

# Point Au Roche (1858)

Point Au Roche was one of the "Three Sisters" constructed by the Lighthouse Service on Lake Champlain in 1858. Similar to Crown Point in New York and Windmill Point in Vermont, these lighthouses were octagonal stone towers with attached Cape Cod-style homes, as keeper's quarters. Point Au Roche was placed opposite La Roche Reef to help vessels altering their course east of the rocky peninsula. The Sixth-Order Fresnel lens, which displayed a fixed white light 54 feet above the lake, was visible for ten miles. In 1934, the Lighthouse Service automated the light, divided the tower from the keeper's quarters and sold the property. The new owner, G. C. Oliver, moved the keeper's quarters north.

Because of the deterioration of the tower, the Coast Guard decided in 1989 that it was no longer safe and moved the light to a buoy on La Roche Reef. Point Au Roche light is adjacent to Monty Bay State Wildlife Management Area on Monty Bay. This light is privately owned and is best seen from Lake Champlain.

Point Au Roche – The Point Au Roche Light is similar to the original Crown Point Light in New York and Windmill Point Light in Vermont. All have an octagonal stone tower, with attached dwellings.

# Barbers Point (1873)

In the late 1780s, Major Hezekiah Barber created one of the first permanent settlements on Lake Champlain at Barber's Point. Located just south of Westport, Barber's Point is midway between Crown Point to the south and Split Rock to the north. Barber operated a ferry that crossed Lake Champlain between Barber's Point on the west shore to Arnold Bay in Panton, Vermont on the eastern shore.

In 1873, a two-story lighthouse structure with a Mansford roof was constructed. The exterior of the lighthouse is finished with blue limestone blocks on the lower portion and white siding on the upper portion and the tower. A Fifth-Order lens, with a focal plane of 83 feet above the lake, beams a fixed white light, which is visible for eleven miles.

In 1935, the Barber's Point Lighthouse was replaced by a steel skeletal tower. The lighthouse and the surrounding property were sold in 1936 and has remained a private residence. A small addition was added to the rear of the lighthouse and a wooden garage stands near the road. The lighthouse has been included it the Camp Dudley Road Historic District and in the National Register of Historic Places.

During their transit, passengers from the steamer, the Curlew, claimed they saw a web-footed creature which has grown to be the legend of Lake Champlain known as "Champ." Barber's Point light, located in Westport just south of Camp Dudley off Route 9N on Barbers Road, is privately owned.

Barbers Point – Legend has it that the first citing of Champ, the creature of Lake Champlain, was at Barbers Point.

# Bluff Point (1874)

Bluff Point Lighthouse is located on a high bluff on the western shore of Valcour Island. In the early morning of October 11, 1776, an American Naval force, under the command of Benedict Arnold, positioned itself on the western side of Valcour Island. Around 10:00 am, the British noticed Benedict Arnold's crew and turned to engage the Americans in what would be the Battle of Lake Champlain, the first naval battle of the Revolutionary War. Arnold realized his fleet was inferior and rather than engaging, he retreated to Schuyler Island. With only two ships damaged, Benedict continued to sail south to Crown Point. The Americans were overtaken near Split Rock, also known as Arnold's Bay. Arnold ran the surviving ships aground, set them on fire, and fled to the south on foot.

Bluff Point was placed in service in 1874 and was the last manned lighthouse on Lake Champlain. The 35-foot tower contained a Fifth-Order lens and was 95 feet above the lake. It could be seen for 13 miles. In 1876, Civil War veteran Major William Herwerth was appointed keeper of Bluff Point Lighthouse. As his health failed, his wife Mary assumed much of the responsibility of tending the light. William passed away on February 17, 1881 and a short time later his wife, Mary, was appointed as the keeper. Mrs. Herwerth had one of the best-kept lighthouses on the lake and faithfully served until 1902.

In 1930, a skeletal tower was erected to replace the manned lighthouse. In 1954, the lighthouse and the land were sold to Dr. Adolph Raboff, a dentist from Massachusetts, who used it as a summer residence. In the 1980s, Dr. Raboff offered the property to the State of New York. After negotiations, a compromise was reached whereby the State would own the lighthouse and Clinton County Historical Association would maintain the structure. Under the leadership of Roger and Linda Harwood, the Clinton County Historical Association restored the lighthouse and helped create several interpretive displays on the lighthouse and its keepers.

In 2001, the New York State Department of Environmental Conservation (DEC) initiated a project to re-light the historic lighthouse. Following discussions between the DEC, Clinton County Historical Association, and the Coast Guard, considerable effort was made to ensure that the lighthouse would help publicize the historic significance of Lake Champlain. In November 2004, the light in the steel tower was returned to its original home in Bluff Point Lighthouse and was re-lit. Today the 1,100-acre Valcour Island is a popular destination for boaters, hikers, anglers, and bird watchers. In addition to the lighthouse, there are more than two dozen campsites, a network of trails, plant communities, and a heron rookery. Bluff Point can be viewed from the marina dock at Day Point or by taking a water taxi from the marina to Valcour Island.

Bluff Point – In 2001, the New York State Department of Environmental Conservation initiated a project to relight the Bluff Point Lighthouse. In 2004, with the assistance of the Clinton County Historical Association and the Coast Guard, the original lamp was restored to the lighthouse and lit.

# Eight - Seaway Trail
## (Lake Erie & Lake Ontario)

**Map 6. Seaway Trail Lighthouses**

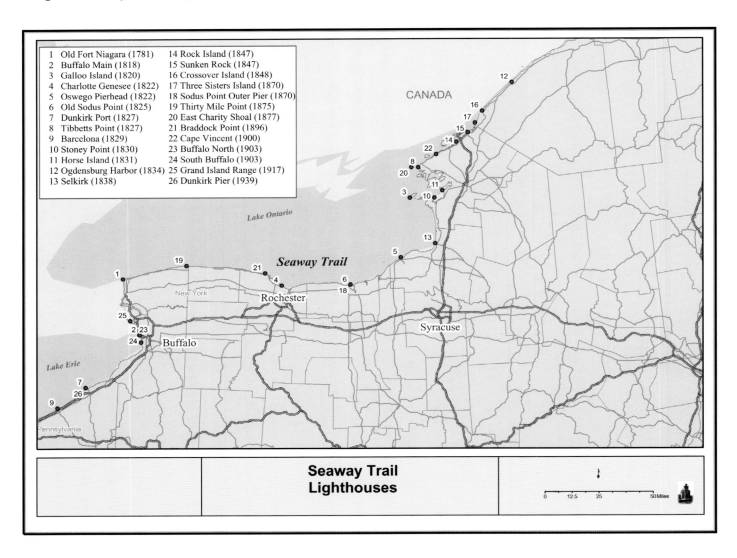

| | |
|---|---|
| 1 Old Fort Niagara (1781) | 14 Rock Island (1847) |
| 2 Buffalo Main (1818) | 15 Sunken Rock (1847) |
| 3 Galloo Island (1820) | 16 Crossover Island (1848) |
| 4 Charlotte Genesee (1822) | 17 Three Sisters Island (1870) |
| 5 Oswego Pierhead (1822) | 18 Sodus Point Outer Pier (1870) |
| 6 Old Sodus Point (1825) | 19 Thirty Mile Point (1875) |
| 7 Dunkirk Port (1827) | 20 East Charity Shoal (1877) |
| 8 Tibbetts Point (1827) | 21 Braddock Point (1896) |
| 9 Barcelona (1829) | 22 Cape Vincent (1900) |
| 10 Stoney Point (1830) | 23 Buffalo North (1903) |
| 11 Horse Island (1831) | 24 South Buffalo (1903) |
| 12 Ogdensburg Harbor (1834) | 25 Grand Island Range (1917) |
| 13 Selkirk (1838) | 26 Dunkirk Pier (1939) |

CANADA

Lake Ontario

*Seaway Trail*

New York

Rochester

Syracuse

Buffalo

Lake Erie

Pennsylvania

**Seaway Trail
Lighthouses**

0    12.5    25    50 Miles

# The Seaway Trail

The Seaway Trail is a scenic gateway that connects the four major waterways in upstate New York: Lake Erie, the Niagara River, Lake Ontario, and the St. Lawrence River. It starts in Erie, Pennsylvania, and extends northeast to Ogdensburg, New York. It is designated as a Recreational Trail and is the longest in America, totaling 454 miles.

The signs are green and white with footprints and a water mark. The Seaway Trail is marked at 42 locations, designating events and battles fought during the War of 1812. The War of 1812 was fought on four fronts: Lake Erie, the Niagara Frontier, Lake Ontario, and along the St. Lawrence River. The first American warship, the Oneida, was built in 1808 on Lake Ontario in Oswego.

Today there are 25 lighthouses along the Seaway Trail. The earliest was constructed at Old Fort Niagara, where a lantern was placed at the top of tower of the Fort in 1781. When the U.S. Postal Service printed commemorative lighthouse stamps of the Great Lakes, they featured the Thirty Mile Point Lighthouse, located 30 miles east of Fort Niagara. Whether traveling by boat or car, the Seaway Trail is an outdoor paradise for camping, boating, fishing, hiking, and reliving the history of America.

# Great Lakes

The Great Lakes have the highest concentration of lighthouses in the **world**. During the history of the Lighthouse Bureau, Lighthouse Service, and Coast Guard, 312 lighthouses were constructed in the United States and Canada. Approximately 200 active lights can be found on the Great Lakes.

With waves comparable to the Atlantic Ocean, often exceeding 40 feet, the Great Lakes can be as treacherous to ships as the Atlantic Ocean. The Great Lakes are notorious for shipwrecks. At least 6,000 ships have been lost on the Great Lakes! The Great Lakes Shipwreck Museum, located at the Whitefish Point Lighthouse in Michigan, contains many artifacts of sunken ships, including the bell and buoys of the *Edmund Fitzgerald*.

The construction of lighthouses on the Great Lakes paralleled the growth of communities in New York State and the nation. Once the Erie Canal and Welland Canal were completed in 1825 and 1829 respectively, an easier nautical passage was possible beyond Lake Ontario. The Welland Canal provided the opportunity to settle the territory beyond the Niagara River and Niagara Falls, west to Lake Erie, Lake Huron, and Lake Michigan. The completed Erie Canal was a gateway to the nation's heartland for millions of immigrants who began to settle the interior of America. In 1855, the shipping canal at Sault St. Marie, Canada linked Lake Superior to the lower four Great Lakes. By the end of the nineteenth century, the Great Lakes had become the single most important transportation system in the United States. Besides grain, lumber and coal, large quantities of iron ore and copper were transported to manufacturing plants in the east. When the Civil War broke out in 1861, the Great Lakes provided the means to spur the nation's economy by transporting natural resources and agricultural goods from America's heartland to the northeast and abroad.

## Great Lakes-
## The Water Bodies and Basins

The Great Lakes are no ordinary lakes. They are the largest fresh water bodies in the world, accounting for 18% of the world's supply. Only the polar ice caps contain more fresh water. The Great Lakes contain 5,500 cubic miles of water, covering a surface area of 94,000 square miles with 11,000 miles of coastline. Both of New York's Great Lakes, Erie and Ontario, have a total of almost 800 miles of coastline. The drainage basin area for both lakes is 68,300 square miles. The retention time is the time it takes water to flow from one end of a water body to another.

|  | Lake Erie | Lake Ontario |
| --- | --- | --- |
| Length | 241 miles | 193 miles |
| Width | 57 miles | 53 miles |
| Average Flow | Lake Erie into Lake Ontario 202,300 cu. ft./sec. | Lake Ontario into St. Lawrence River 239,700 cu. ft./sec. |
| Average Depth | 62 ft. | 283 ft. |
| Maximum Depth | 210 ft. | 802 ft. |
| Retention Time | 2.6 days | 6 days |

Table 2 - Comparison of Lake Erie and Lake Ontario

# Old Fort Niagara
# (1782, 1823, 1872)

Fort Niagara, located at the mouth of the Niagara River on Lake Ontario, was established by the French fur traders in 1726. In 1759, the British took possession of Fort Niagara, one of the most valued prizes from the French and Indian Wars. Historians believe that in 1781, the first lighthouse on the Great Lakes was built approximately 100 yards away from Old Fort Niagara. The British who held the Fort built a tower on the roof of the store building, called the castle, and installed a simple whale oil lamp that remained there until about 1803. A second beacon, constructed in 1822 atop the castle, remained until 1872.

The importance of Fort Niagara was greatly diminished when Canada opened the Welland Canal in 1829. This canal encouraged traffic further west to the fastest growing city of Buffalo. The light in place today was built in 1872. It is a four-story, rough gray stone octagonal tower with an attached watch house. The tower is accented with beautiful arch windows on each level. On top of the fourth level is band of miniature windows with its own arch. The original tower was extended in 1900 using brick to include the new miniature windows and base for the new lantern room. The lantern room is surrounded by a black railing and has a metal roof, topped with a ventilator ball. The lantern was extinguished in June 1993 after operating more than 120 years. The lighthouse can be viewed at the entrance to Fort Niagara and can accessed by traveling north on Robert Moses Parkway from Niagara Falls.

Figure 8-1. Buffalo Depot

Old Fort Niagara – Constructed in 1872, the current lighthouse was active until 1993.

### Fort Niagara

Old Fort Niagara stands on a hill near the entrance to the Niagara River. Located in Old Fort Niagara State Historic Site, the light is part of the New York State Office of Parks, Recreation and Historic Preservation. With a history that spans over 300 years, Fort Niagara Light is a National Historic Landmark. The facility contains the most complete collection of eighteenth century military architecture in the country. Old Fort Niagara is the site of many monthly historic re-enactments and celebrations. Regular programming at the Fort includes soldiers on duty, musket firing, eighteenth century cooking, and Old Fort Niagara Guard drills with musket and cannon firings. For a complete list of events, visit http://www.oldfortniagara.org/ or contact the New York State Office of Parks, Recreation and Historic Preservation.

# Buffalo Main (1818, 1833)

Many signal lights have marked the entrance to the Buffalo Harbor, which became one of the busiest ports in America. These included nine lighthouses and one lightship. Congress appropriated money for a lighthouse in Buffalo as early as 1805.

Construction of the first tower was delayed until 1818 because of the damage Buffalo suffered from the British attacks in the War of 1812. After the Erie Canal was completed in 1825, ship traffic into Buffalo, located at the western end of the canal, increased significantly. By the late 1800s, Buffalo became one of the busiest ports in America and was the seventh busiest port in the world, receiving more than 100 ships per day. The current Buffalo Main Light, built in 1833 to replace the original light, is the second oldest structure in Buffalo. Also known as Chinaman's Light, the Buffalo Light is 68-feet tall, is octagonal in shape, and is made of gray limestone. In 1851, the tower was heightened to 76 feet and in 1853, $2,500 was appropriated for a fog bell. The bell was never delivered; instead a new lighting chandelier was purchased in 1854, reducing the arc of illumination from 180 degrees to 110 degrees, but increasing the intensity. In 1856, a fog bell and a Third-Order Fresnel lens with fixed white light were installed. In order to replace the lens, the old lantern was removed, new casement windows were added, a two-story metal top was built, and a platinum-tipped copper lighting rod was installed.

The old landmark Chinaman's Light, part of a busy U.S. Coast Guard Station in the 1950s, was used as a storage facility for explosives. In 1962, when the last three Coast Guardsmen were relieved from the south Buffalo entrance, the light was automated. Chinaman's Light was temporarily relit with a flood-light for the nation's bicentennial, and in 1979 it was included on National Register of Historic Places.

Buffalo Main – The Buffalo Main Light (1833) is the second oldest structure in the city of Buffalo. In 1851, the tower was heightened to seventy-six feet above the lake level.

The Buffalo Lighthouse Association was formed in 1985 to undertake major structural restoration of the tower. The Association also signed a 30-year license with the Coast Guard. After the tower was restored and the replacement lens was installed, the lighthouse was relit in 1987 for the first international Friendship Festival. The City of Buffalo, the Coast Guard, and the Lighthouse Association have developed a beautiful waterfront park with public gardens and a floating naval museum.

Buffalo Main Lighthouse is located on the Coast Guard station. To view the light take I-90 to the Church Street exit. Turn right at the first light on Lower Terrace and proceed to the waterfront park.

Buffalo Main – The first two lights on the Great Lakes were the Buffalo Main Light in New York and Presque Isle Light in Erie, Pennsylvania.

# Galloo Island (1820, 1867)

Galloo Island, located 16 miles from Sackets Harbor, marks the outer border of a group of islands that guard Sackets Harbor and the entrance to the St. Lawrence River. The present tower, constructed in 1867, is a 55-foot tall, conical shaped structure, with an attached one and one-half story keeper's dwelling. Both are constructed of cut gray limestone, quarried on the island.

The lighthouse was automated in 1963 and was added to the National Register of Historic Places on April 8, 1983. The round, copper lantern room has turned green from exposure to the air, and surrounds an automated beacon. A square iron house, which contained the fog signal, is 350 feet southwest of the lighthouse. The New York State Department of Environmental Conservation owns 25 acres surrounding the former light station. Nearly all the rest of the island, a total of 1937 acres, was purchased at an auction in 1999, making it the second largest private island in the United States. The nearby Coast Guard Station has been abandoned.

To view the lighthouse, travel from Henderson or Sackets Harbor about ten miles out into Lake Ontario to Galloo Island. The light is on the southern end of the island.

Galloo Island – This light sits on 1,037 acres and is the second largest privately-owned island in America.

# Charlotte-Genesee (1822)

Congress established the Port of Genesee in 1805 and a collector was appointed for this new customs district, since Charlotte was a hub for coal and wheat production. In 1821, the U.S. government purchased 3.75-acres of land from Mehitabel Hincher. Seven months later, an octagonal limestone tower lighthouse was erected on a bluff, overlooking the western bank of the Genesee River and Port of Rochester. The stone tower is capped with a ten-sided lantern room that has a black steel roof and a ventilator ball.

Because of the shifting sands at the mouth of the Genesee River, piers were constructed in 1829 to help define the inlet and improve the navigation entering the port. Over time, the piers were lengthened and the beach grew, causing the lighthouse to be removed from the water's edge. In 1863, the keeper's house was replaced with the current red brick house. By 1881, the Lighthouse Service removed it from operation, although the residence was used by its personnel. The keeper's house was used by a civilian keeper until 1940 when the property was transferred to the Coast Guard.

In the 1965, the light was considered surplus property by the Coast Guard and plans were made to tear it down. It was saved by the efforts of Charlotte High School students. Interestingly, the architect used the lighthouse as an inspiration when he designed their high school. The students rallied in support of the lighthouse and launched a successful letter writing campaign to save the lighthouse.

Charlotte-Genesee is now leased to the Charlotte-Genesee Lighthouse Historical Society. During the annual Rediscovery Day celebration in 1984, the lamp was relit to shine over the shores of Lake Ontario. The Lighthouse Museum and tower are open to the public on weekend afternoons from May to Mid-October, and the grounds are open daily. To find this lighthouse, travel along Lake Shore Boulevard to Lake Avenue, north to Holy Cross Church. There is a parking lot available behind the church.

Charlotte Genesee – The original keeper's quarters now serves as a museum. In 1984, the lamp was relit to shine over the shores of Lake Ontario.

# Oswego West Pierhead
## (1822, 1834)

The first lighthouse in Oswego was constructed in 1822, on the grounds of Fort Ontario, near the eastern shore of the Oswego River. The original keeper's house can still be viewed at the fort. The second light, an octagonal gray stone tower with an attached oil room, was erected in 1836 at the end of the west pier. This structure lasted nearly 100 years before it was torn down in 1930. As a testament to its endurance, a mural of the lighthouse was painted inside the Oswego City Savings Bank on West First Street.

Today's lighthouse was built in 1934 at the end of a new stone pier. It is a simple square structure with an attached tower. It contains a rotating red tinted Fourth-Order lens that is visible for ten miles. Several Coast Guardsmen were killed in 1942 during a boating accident while changing keepers. Oswego was automated shortly after the accident and remains in service today.

A wonderful collection of lighthouse and maritime history can be viewed at the H. Lee White Maritime Museum, located in Oswego Harbor The lighthouse is owned and operated by the Oswego Coast Guard Station and can be seen from the museum parking lot. Another historic treasure which is located within two miles of the light is the Erie Canal Barge System. Visitors can view three locks along the Oswego River.

To visit the light, take Route 104 (the Seaway Trail) in Oswego, turn north onto West First Street, turn left on Van Buren, and bear right onto Lake Street. Drive onto the pier to get a good view of the light. There is a small marina west of the pier that also offers a good view of the lighthouse. The lighthouse itself is not accessible.

Oswego Pierhead – The pierhead light is located on a rock pier that is over 0.5 mile long. The current lighthouse was built in 1934 and has a rotating red lamp that is visible for fifteen miles.

Oswego Pierhead – The harbor is a peaceful location to watch the sun set over Lake Ontario.

# Old Sodus Point (1825, 1870)

In 1824, local residents and lake captains joined together to establish a lighthouse in Great Sodus Bay. The first piers were erected in 1824 at the entrance to the bay and a beacon was placed at the end. Construction of a rough split stone tower and keeper's quarters was completed a year later. It is similar in design to the Oswego and Charlotte-Genesee lighthouses. The first lighthouse was replaced because of the extensive repairs that were needed.

The current 45-foot tower was constructed in 1870 of limestone from Kingston, Ontario. In 1901, the Lighthouse Service determined that the newer beacon, a Fourth-Order Fresnel lens, was sufficient and they extinguished the original 1825 shore light. The keeper's quarters, a two-and-one half story dwelling, was actively used by the Lighthouse Service and later by the Coast Guard until 1984.

Today the Old Sodus Lighthouse is on both the New York and National Historic Registers and is leased by the Sodus Bay Historical Society. The lighthouse is now known as the Sodus Bay Lighthouse Museum and the keeper's residence houses the maritime museum, gift shop, and library. The 1870 tower still houses the original Fresnel lens, which flashes every six seconds. During the summer, the Historical Society holds many events including concerts, a 5-K race, flea markets and cookouts. The outer Sodus Bay Light is an automated red light that guides many boats into Sodus Bay. To visit the light, travel north on Route 14 and turn on to Ontario Street at the Fire Hall.

Old Sodus Point – During the summer, the Sodus Bay Historical Society hosts many events on the grounds of the lighthouse.

# Dunkirk Port
## (1827, 1857, 1875)

Point Gratiot is located on a bluff overlooking Lake Erie and Dunkirk Harbor and has assisted many ships to safely navigate Lake Erie. Point Gratiot is believed to be named after Charles Gratiot, the same U.S. Army engineer for whom Fort Gratiot, on Michigan's St. Clair River, is named. Dunkirk Port is located at the western end of the Erie Canal and was first built in 1827. It was rebuilt in 1857 due to erosion and in 1875, a new Victorian-style keeper's dwelling was constructed. The lighthouse tower originally housed a Third-Order lens whose focal plane height was 82 feet and was visible for 12 miles. A short passage way led to a circular staircase that was built inside the tower to access the lantern room. At the top of the tower, a square metal railing surrounded the ten-sided lantern. The red metal base matched the curved roof and ventilator ball.

Dunkirk Port was the site of many unfortunate shipwrecks. Two of the most memorable were the *Dean Richmond* and the *Idaho*. In 1893 the steamboat *Dean Richmond*, which carried sacks of meal, flour, copper sheet, and gold and silver bullion, sank off Dunkirk. Dunkirk residents salvaged hundreds of bags of damp flour after the wreck. In 1897, the freighter *Idaho* was lost. Some of *Idaho's* cargo which included slabs of chocolate was recovered by the locals. Dunkirk Port also played a part in America's history. The first shot fired during the War of 1812 came from the banks of Point Gratiot. During World War II, twelve Coast Guardsmen and a keeper were stationed at the lighthouse.

Dunkirk Port – The first shot fired during the War of 1812 were from the banks of Port Gratiot. Today, the lighthouse is home of Veterans Park Museum which has an extensive collection of military artifacts.

A white bottle-shaped beacon pier light at the entrance to welcomes visitors to Veteran's Park. This bottle beacon is one of two lights that were used along the Seaway Trail. The other one is now on the grounds of the Buffalo Coast Guard station, adjacent to the Buffalo Main Light. Bottle beacons are constructed of boilerplate, are about 30 feet high, have four distinguished cast iron port windows, and a curved iron door. They usually have the smallest Sixth-Order lens.

Today, the lighthouse is the home of the Veteran's Park Museum which contains an extensive collection of military artifacts. During the month of August, Veteran's Park hosts a popular Tall Ships Visitation and Re-enactment of the War of 1812. The lighthouse complex is located south of Dunkirk, off Route 15, which parallels the shore of Lake Erie.

Dunkirk Port – A Third-Order Fresnel lens in the tower at Dunkirk Light.

# Tibbetts Point (1827, 1854)

Tibbetts Point Lighthouse marks the point where the Saint Lawrence River meets Lake Ontario. Once part of a 600-acre parcel belonging to Captain John Tibbett, a three-acre site was deeded to the government, who erected a 59-foot stone lighthouse in 1827. The lighthouse tower was equipped with a 50-candlepower oil lamp and a Fourth-Order Fresnel lens. Later the oil lamps were removed and replaced with a 500-watt, 15,000-candlepower lamp that used a Fourth-Order lens. A steam-operated fog whistle was added in 1896 and in 1927 the whistle was upgraded to an air diaphone fog signal. In 1854, the present 69-foot light tower was erected with the Fourth-Order lens.

The buildings at the lighthouse parcel include a two-story keeper's residence, a steam fog signal building, a one story brick building for the two air compressors (1927), and an iron oil house. The complex served as a Coast Guard Station until 1981.

Tibbetts Point – A view from the tower and the fourth-order lens.

Tibbetts Point – The buildings at the lighthouse complex include a keepers quarters, a fog signal building, and an iron oil house. The complex at Tibbetts Point served as a Coast Guard station until 1981. In 1988, the Tibbetts Point Lighthouse Society was formed. Today the site is an American Youth Hostel and a wonderful place to meet travelers from around the world.

In 1988, the Tibbetts Point Lighthouse Society was formed and was responsible for restoring and preserving the station. The site is now an American Youth Hostel. A visitor's center and museum opened on the site in 1993 and the grounds are open for public use. The light is still an active aid to navigation and is the only operating Fresnel lens on Lake Ontario. To find this picturesque site, travel along Route 12F from Watertown to Cape Vincent. Take a left turn (south) onto Broadway and travel 2.5 miles to the Tibbetts Point Lighthouse.

## Barcelona (1829)

The Barcelona Lighthouse was the first building in the United States to be illuminated by natural gas. Originally the tower was illuminated by eleven lamps fueled with oil. In 1828, the government designated Portland Harbor (now Barcelona) on Lake Erie as a port of entry and appropriated funds to construct a lighthouse. William Hart, a local gunsmith and entrepreneur worked to lay two miles of hollowed wooden pipes to provide natural gas as the energy source for the lighthouse for the next nine years. Eventually, due to the quality of the gas, the light was reverted back to oil.

The lighthouse tower and keeper's dwelling were completed in 1829. They are made of native split stone with a 40-foot tower and a 22-foot diameter base. Because a railroad was built along the lakeshore in 1852, Barcelona never grew into a major port. The lighthouse was decommissioned in 1859 by the Lighthouse Service when it realized Barcelona did possess a harbor. In 1872, the tower, quarters, and property were sold at an auction to George Patterson. The light remained extinguished until 1962 when a new gas beacon was installed. Faith Patterson Scott, a fifth generation Scott, owned the property until she passed away.

In 1998, after 126 years of ownership by the Scott family Bruce and Ann Mulkin took possession of the lighthouse. To view the lighthouse, travel the New York State Thruway (I-90) to East Lake Road (Route 5) in Barcelona.

Barcelona – Barcelona was the first lighthouse in America converted to natural gas in 1831 by William Hart, who also built the gas lines to light the Village of Fredonia. The lighthouse was connected to a natural gas supply by two miles of wooden pipe.

# Stoney Point (1830, 1869)

Stoney Point is on an anvil-like peninsula at the entrance to Henderson Bay and Harbor. The first lighthouse was erected in 1830 to mark the entrance to Henderson Harbor. The foundation of the original lighthouse structure is still visible to visitors. The current lighthouse was constructed in 1869 and is similar in design to Horse Island. The 69-foot tower is attached to the two-story keepers dwelling. The tower was decommissioned in 1947 and sold as a private residence. In 1966, a fire in a nearby barn damaged the lighthouse, but the structure was restored by the owners. It is located on Lighthouse Road in Henderson Harbor. Access is limited, as it sits on private property.

Stoney Point – Located near the entrance to Henderson harbor, the current lighthouse was built in 1869 and stands sixty-nine feet above lake level.

# Horse Island (1831, 1870)

Horse Island is located at the entrance to Sackets Harbor, the nation's most important shipbuilding center during the War of 1812. Sackets Harbor was the Great Lakes Headquarters for the U. S. Navy. One third of the U.S. Army and one quarter of the Navy were stationed here during the war. The harbor was the site of two major battles during the war, and Horse Island was the staging area for the British Navy's second battle on May 29, 1813. Under Colonel Backus, the U. S. Light Dragons helped to defend Sackets Harbor until the war's end.

The first lighthouse was built at this important military post in 1831. The present structure was built in 1870. The 50-foot tower, similar in design to Stoney Point Lighthouse, was replaced by a skeleton tower in 1957. The lighthouse is privately owned, but can be viewed by boat, and is visible from the Sackets Harbor Battlefield.

Horse Island – This island is located at entrance to Sackets Harbor, which was an important ship building center during the War of 1812. The harbor was headquarters for the Navy and one-third of the U.S. Army.

# Ogdensburg Harbor
# (1834, 1900)

The site of the Ogdensburg Harbor Lighthouse was once the setting for the first permanent settlement in New York State. A French missionary, Francis Piquet, established a mission fort at the mouth of River La Presentation (now Oswegatchie River) in 1749. Fort La Presentation was built to convert the Native Americans and to control the passage between the Great Lakes and Montreal. Ogdensburg was a site for a battle on February 4, 1813, between the British and American troops. During the battle, the U.S. troops were captured. U.S. prisoners were freed from a local jail, taking 52 British prisoners and a supply of muskets. The British retaliated by marching 600 troops and a militia with cannons to Ogdensburg where they captured 50 American prisoners.

The original Ogdensburg Light was built in 1834 and was refitted in 1870. It is a similar design to Stoney Point and Horse Island Lights. The existing lighthouse, a stone cut structure, one and a half stories high, includes an attached 65-foot tower. In 1900, the current lighthouse was refitted and the tower was raised to its current height. The lighthouse was decommissioned in the 1960s and is no longer active. To reach the lighthouse, travel on Route 68 (Canton Street) and turn left on Riverside Avenue. It is privately owned and only opened upon request.

Ogdensburg Harbor – At one time, the site for the Ogdensburg lighthouse was the location for Fort LaPresentation, which was built in 1749.

# Selkirk (Salmon River) (1838)

The government purchased approximately 5,760 square feet of land for the Port Ontario Lighthouse Reservation from Sylvester and Daniel Brown on September 1, 1837. Originally called the Salmon River Light Station, the lighthouse was constructed in 1838 for $3,000. From the 1849 Light List, the record noted that the original light was identical to Horse Island, which had fourteen-inch diameter parabolic reflectors with eight lamps. The lamps burned whale oil from a twenty-four-hour reservoir and use a frost lamp during the cold weather to warm up the main lamp. The 1858 Light List notes that lamp system was upgraded to a Hains Mineral Oil fountain lamp with a single burner, 270-degree Sixth-Order Fresnel lens.

The light was operated only during shipping season and keeper's salary was $350 for the eight to nine months of duty. The lighthouse was deactivated in 1858, although Coast Guard records indicate that the station was still an active Life-Saving Station on April 1, 1877. Records after the de-activation showed that Lucius Cole resided there from 1852 until his death in 1890. After Cole's death, the Life Saving Service Stations on the Great Lakes were closed during the depression in 1893.

A German hotelier from Syracuse, named Leopold Jon, purchased the Selkirk Lighthouse for $155 in 1895. Leopold acquired the adjoining properties and developed the site into a successful resort for visitors from Syracuse and even as far away as Philadelphia. After Leopold's unexpected death in 1907, the Heckle family purchased the property in 1916.

The Selkirk Lighthouse was dedicated as a "Designated Historic Landmark" by the Oswego Heritage Foundation in November 1976 and was elected to the National Register of Historic Places in March 1979. During a Bicentennial celebration on August 6, 1989, the lighthouse was relit using a Coast Guard-approved, photocell-actuated lamp with auto bulb changer. Today the lighthouse is owned and operated by Jim Walker and guest accommodations are available. To view the lighthouse, follow Route 3 to Port Ontario and take Lake Road to the end.

Selkirk – Built at the mouth of the Salmon River in 1838, in 1989, the light was relit after many years of being inactive.

# Rock Island (1847, 1882)

Rock Island is one of six lighthouses on the St. Lawrence River and is the only light on the Seaway that has retained its tower and all its auxiliary structures. The 1882 lighthouse replaced the combination lighthouse and keeper's house of 1847. The lighthouse complex includes a fieldstone smoke house, generator house (1900), boathouse (1920), carpenter's shop (1882) and keeper's house. The current tower is located on a smaller rock closer to the water's edge.

Of all the keepers, Bill Johnson and Frank Ward were the most noteworthy. Bill Johnson was reportedly a pirate in his former days. Frank Ward was the last keeper at Rock Island and was stationed at the facility from 1938 to 1941. His duties included tending to several battery-operated lights. Ward was also stationed at the Crossover Island prior to Rock Island Lighthouse. His widow remembers countless incidents of search and rescue made by her husband. Ward helped to save the life of a man whose companion had drowned. As a result of that rescue, Mr. Ward became sick and never regained full health.

Today, Rock Island Light is owned by New State Office of Parks and Historic Preservation and is operated by the Thousand Island Park Commission. A citizen's group from Wellesley Island raised funds to maintain the tower and volunteers from the group manicure the lawn, plant flowers, and supervise the tower. It is open to the public and there are picnic facilities on the island. Visitors may travel to the island by public water taxi from Fishers Landing, off Route 12 in the Town of Alexandria.

Rock Island – This is the only lighthouse on the St. Lawrence that has retained its tower and all its auxiliary structures. Rock Island is easily accessible by water taxi, open as a day use park, and is owned by New York State Office Parks and Historic Preservation.

# Sunken Rock (1847)

One of the author's favorite lighthouses on the Seaway Trail is located on Bush Island, which marks the east entrance to the narrows between Wellesley Island and the mainland. Constructed in 1847 and refitted in 1855, the tower is sheathed with white boards. The island's other building served as a boat-house and one-room keeper's dwelling. The lighthouse is situated a picturesque setting near Heart Island and Boldt Castle. Boldt Castle was conceived by George Boldt, the owner of the Waldorf-Astoria Hotel in New York. He built the castle as sign of his love for his wife Louise. In 1904, before the castle was completed, Louise died and Mr. Boldt never finished the dream.

Keeper Horace Walts served at both Sisters Island and Sunken Rock lights. Mr. Walts received nine stars for outstanding service, and a permanent gold star with a diamond. The light is an active aid to navigation and is owned by St. Lawrence Development Corporation. In 1988, the light was converted to solar energy with solar panels and storage batteries. Visitors can view the Sunken Rock Lighthouse from the waterfront in downtown Alexandria Bay.

Sunken Rock – Owned by the St. Lawrence development Corporation, in 1988, this light was converted to solar energy with solar panels and storage batteries. It is built on an artificial island to mark a dangerous submerged rock.

# Crossover Island (1848, 1882)

The Crossover Island Lighthouse was named after the ships that crossed over between the American and Canadian Channel at the point near the island. It was constructed in 1848 and rebuilt in 1882. The keeper's house was patterned after the Tibbetts Point design. The lighthouse complex on the island consists of a six-room keeper's house, steel tower with a Sixth-Order lens, oil house, a hen house, barn, privy, and an ash house. The boat house was built in 1869 and rebuilt after a fire in 1890.

Daniel Hill, who served as a keeper from 1909 to 1931, was stationed at Buffalo Reef, Thirty Mile Point, Ogdensburg, Huron, and Crossover Island. Mr. Hill recorded over 400 rescues! One of his most dramatic rescues included saving three passengers of a biplane that had crashed near the island. After the passengers were brought safely ashore, the plane exploded and burned.

Ralph Hill, son of Keeper Daniel Hill, wrote many articles for the Thousand Island Sun and also wrote two books about living with his family at the lighthouse. The keeper's four children attended a one-room schoolhouse on the mainland. Their father made the 1.5 mile roundtrip rowing across the channel in all weather conditions. This island was known for the millions of eel flies, which reproduced each June. According to one of Ralph Hill's writings, the Hill family harvested 200 eels nightly. The family would skin and clean them for smoking the next day.

The light was discontinued in 1942 and in 1960, the island was sold as surplus property. Today the light has been replaced by a nearby skeleton tower. The island is privately owned and serves as a summer residence. The light is visible from the scenic overlook on Route 12, east of Chippewa Bay.

Crossover Island – Daniel Hill served as keeper from 1909 to 1930 at Buffalo Reef, Thirty Mile Point, Ogdensburg, and Crossover Island. As a keeper, Mr. Hill saved over 400 lives!

# Three Sisters Island (1870)

The Three Sisters Island Lighthouse is located approximately 12.5 miles northeast of Alexandria Bay, in the St. Lawrence River. Once three separate islands, the islands are now joined together. The lighthouse and a neighboring shed are the only structures on the Three Sisters Island. The lighthouse was built to mark a difficult channel on the Canadian side of the island. After nine years of negotiation, the lighthouse was built in 1870. After the commissioning of the lighthouse, the channel alignment was moved to the American side of the island. In order to accomplish this hazardous task, divers drilled holes in the bedrock and blasted the bedrock with dynamite. Working from a support barge, a thunder and lightning storm detonated the dynamite and killed nine crewmembers.

William Dodge, a Civil War veteran, was the first keeper and he was replaced by his son. The Dodge family served at the Three Sisters Island light for 51 years.

The Three Sisters Island is the site of many shipwrecks. In 1890, the passenger steamship Ocean collided with the barge *Kent*. The Dodges were awakened by a violent crash as the *Ocean* hit the Three Sisters Island rocks. The captain of the *Ocean* had been steaming his vessel at full speed in the shallow island waters. Close by, at Upper Brother Island, a coal-ship strayed from the channel, struck the island, and sunk. It remains at the bottom of the river.

Another picturesque island adjacent to Three Sisters is Dark Island, named after the thick dense evergreens. Dark Island was home to the Chippewa Indians, who named the region Manatonna (Garden of the Great Spirit). Around 1900, Frederick Bourne, the head of the Singer Sewing Machine Company, bought the island and built Jordstat Castle. Jordstat Castle rivaled the Boldt Castle and the castles along the Rhine River in Germany. The castle is made of granite quarried from nearby Oak Island.

With the opening of the St. Lawrence Seaway in 1959, the light was replaced with a nearby buoy. Today, the light is a private residence and is no longer active. The Three Sisters Island light cannot be viewed from the mainland, but can be seen by boat, from either Chippewa or Alexandria Bay.

Three Sisters Island – The channel near the light was moved to the American side of the island after the lighthouse was built in 1870. To alter the alignment, a crew used dynamite to blast the underwater rock. During a storm, the dynamite, stored on a barge, was accidentally detonated and nine crewmembers were killed.

## Buffalo Lightship

In 1912, Lightship No. 82 was built in Muskegon, Michigan by the Racine-Truscott-Shell Lake Boat Company. The 80-foot, steel-hulled vessel had a beam width of 21 feet and room for six crewmen. On deck, the lightship had a main lantern mast in the front of the ship, supporting three kerosene-fueled lanterns. The vessel also had a ten-inch, steam-powered fog whistle. On August 3, 1912, the Bureau of Lighthouses used four-ton anchors to firmly position the lightship off Point Albino, which was 13 miles west of Buffalo Harbor. Although the lightship was stationed in Canadian waters, the Bureau of Lighthouses maintained the vessel.

At the time the Buffalo Lightship assumed her post, only one other lightship had ever sunk in the United States. Lightship No. 37, stationed off Five Fathom Bank, New Jersey, was sunk during a hurricane in August 1893. Most mariners on the Great Lakes considered freshwater lightships unsinkable. But on November 8, 1913, an unprecedented weather pattern would determine the Buffalo Lightship's fate. That day, two low-pressure systems collided over Lake Superior, generating blizzard conditions. A third low-pressure system swept northward toward Lake Erie, producing tremendous winds and snowfall at the storm's center, which developed further west on Lake Huron. In total, ten ships and 238 sailors were lost in this storm, which included the crew of the Buffalo Lightship.

Figure 8-2. Buffalo Lightship

A cursory search around Point Albino revealed no lightship. The inspector for the Tenth Lighthouse District became worried and ordered the launch of a formal search.

Several days after the storm, a Buffalo resident discovered a life preserver inscribed with the words "Lightship No. 82." This was the first tangible clue that the lightship had sunk. Soon after a small piece of wood was found with the words "Good-bye Nellie, the ship is breaking up fast. Williams." The message is believed to have been written by Captain Williams to his wife. The wreck of the Buffalo Lightship was not discovered until the following spring. The Bureau of Lighthouses raised her in the fall of 1915. The ship was quite damaged but was rebuilt and used as a relief ship in Lake Michigan.

# Sodus Point Outer Pier
## (1870, 1901, 1938)

Piers were built in Sodus Bay in 1834, nine years after the Old Sodus Point shore light became active. At that time a minor beacon was placed at the end of the entrance to the bay. It was replaced in 1858 and the first permanent light on the piers was added in 1870. An inner pier light, added in 1895, was later torn down. The beacon was improved in 1901, and replaced in 1938 by the current 45-foot tall white pierhead light. The limestone shore light of 1870 was decommissioned in 1901. From 1901 to 1984, the keeper's residence housed the personnel who maintained the pierhead light. Today Sodus Outer Light is automated and its red lantern still guides vessels into Sodus Bay. The pierhead light is located near the Old Sodus Light. The Outer Pier Light is located off Bay Street at the end of Wickham Avenue. The lighthouse pier is a great location to fish or just watch the sunset over Lake Ontario.

Sodus Point Outer Pier – Sodus Point Outer Pier is picturesque location for sunsets and fishing. The Pier light was automated in the 1980s.

# Thirty Mile Point (1875)

Thirty Mile Point Lighthouse is located 30 miles east of the mouth of the Niagara River, which empties in Lake Ontario. The lighthouse was constructed in 1875 to mark a sandbar and shoal located offshore. At least four boats have been lost near the point. The most notable was the vessel from French explorer, Sieur de la Salle, in 1678. In 1780, the *Ontario*, carrying British troops and an army payroll of $15,000 sank near Thirty Mile Point. There were no survivors. In 1817, another ship, the *Mary*, also sank in the area.

The lighthouse is constructed of hand-carved limestone, is 70 feet high, and contains a Third-Order Fresnel lens. A climb up the circular staircase to the light tower offers a panoramic view across the lake to Canada. The lantern first used kerosene. In 1885, the light was electrified.

The original keeper's house was designed to accommodate a single family, but was later expanded to house two families. The Coast Guard assumed control of the station in 1935 and added a fog signal. By 1958, the shoal and the sandbar eroded away and the lighthouse was extinguished. A skeleton tower was built nearby to replace the light.

In the late 1950s and early 1960s, New York State began to purchase farms and properties on Lower Lake Road. In 1962, the area was dedicated as Golden Hill State Park. The lighthouse, located in Golden Hill State Park, most likely acquired its name from the goldenrod that once bloomed on a nearby island. However, some say that the name comes from the lost gold and silver from the sunken ships, *Ontario* and *Mary*.

Thirty Mile Point – Located thirty miles east of Ft. Niagara, the keepers quarters is a great beacon for lodging. It contains three bedrooms, one bath, kitchen, living room, and a private entrance.

Although the lighthouse was still owned by the Coast Guard, the deed was signed over to New York State Office of Parks, Recreation and Historic Preservation in October 1984. Today the lighthouse is the centerpiece of Golden Hill State Park. Nearby are 50 campsites, picnic shelters, a marina, and nature trails. A new feature was added in 2001. The former keeper's quarters on the second floor are available for rent. The "Lighthouse Cottage" consists of three bedrooms, full bath, kitchen, a beautiful living room, and a private entrance. A marvelous view of Lake Ontario from the second floor is available year round. The lighthouse is also open on weekends with limited afternoon hours. To confirm hours, contact the campsite office. To reach Golden Hills State Park, take Route 18 to Route 269 (north) and west on Lake Road.

# East Charity Shoal (1877, 1935)

East Charity Shoal, a cast-iron light, was originally constructed in Vermillion, Ohio, in 1877. The lighthouse was on the verge of collapse after a severe ice storm. The Lighthouse Board had the structure removed and transported to Buffalo in 1929. In 1935, the restored 16-foot tower was rebuilt and placed on East Charity Shoal. The lighthouse was constructed on a pile of rocks, has a focal plane of 52 feet, and is still in use today, helping ships navigate Lake Ontario. Visitors can view the light from Cape Vincent on a clear day with the help of a telescope.

East Charity Shoal – The tower at East Charity Shoal was originally constructed in Vermillion, Ohio, in 1877. In 1935, the tower was rebuilt and placed at East Charity Shoal.

# Braddock Point (1896)

The Braddock Point Lighthouse is a copy of an old Cleveland lighthouse that was torn down in 1895. The ornate brass lantern, Fresnel lens, and the metal works were taken from Cleveland and used to finish Braddock Point. The lighthouse was constructed in 1896 and included a Victorian keeper's house and 110-foot octagonal brick tower. Twice each day, the keeper climbed the circular staircase, which included 118 steps, to maintain the brightest lighthouse on Lake Ontario. The tower contained a Three and One-half Order Fresnel lens and a 20,000-candle power lamp that could be seen up to eighteen miles away. For 57 years, the lighthouse was operated by the Lighthouse Board and then the Coast Guard. The light was extinguished on January 1, 1954 and the upper two-thirds of the tower were removed by the Coast Guard because of structural damage.

In 1957, the lighthouse was purchased by a couple for a summer home. After moving in, the owners decided to live there year round. They restored the keeper's house, the carriage house and remaining portion of the shortened tower. The magnificent property was sold to a second owner who, enjoy the spacious grounds. Braddock Point Lighthouse is located at the end of Lighthouse Road, which is off Lake Ontario Parkway. The lighthouse is private property and should not be accessed without prior permission.

Braddock Point – In the dead of winter, visiting Braddock Point is a bone chilling experience. The original tower at Braddock Point had 118 steps in the circular, spiral staircase. In 1954, the tower was shortened by the Coast Guard because of structural problems.

# Cape Vincent Breakwater (1900)

A small square lighthouse welcomes visitors who approach Cape Vincent from the south on Route 12 E. The lighthouse was one of two lights that were erected at the end of the village break wall. The lighthouses were constructed in 1900 and deactivated in 1934. One of the remaining lights was moved to its present location in 1951. The white wooden tower stands 15 feet high and is topped with a square black parapet and an octagonal lantern room. The Tibbetts Point Lighthouse is near the Cape Vincent Breakwater and is feasible to visit both in one day.

Cape Vincent – The lighthouse serves as a great welcome to visitors approaching Cape Vincent. The tower was originally located at the end of break wall in the St. Lawrence River.

# Buffalo North Breakwater (1903)

Also known as Buffalo Bottle Light, this light is located in Parkland near the Buffalo Main Light, at the south entrance to the Buffalo River at the Coast Guard Station. The Buffalo North Breakwater was constructed in 1903. This 29-foot bottle beacon is one of two lights that were used along the Seaway Trail. The other one is on the grounds of the Dunkirk Light Station. In 1960, a Sixth-Order Fresnel lens was installed and the lighthouse was automated. The light was deactivated in 1985. The light is located near the Coast Guard Station at the Buffalo Main Lighthouse. To view this lighthouse, take Interstate 90 to Church Street. Turn right at the first light on lower Terrace. Proceed to the Waterfront Park.

Buffalo North – Also know as the Buffalo "Bottle Light," it is similar to the bottle light at the Dunkirk Light Station.

# South Buffalo (1903)

The South Buffalo Lighthouse is a round, 30-foot tall steel structure on the end of an industrial pier near the south entrance to the harbor. It was constructed in 1903 and has a circular black base that rises to support a white tower. The lantern room has diamond shaped panes and focal plane of 43 feet. This lighthouse was automated in 1935 and is located approximately 1.2 miles south of the Buffalo Main Lighthouse. It can be viewed off the Tift Street, off Fuhrmann Boulevard.

South Buffalo – Constructed in 1903, the light is located at the south entrance to the harbor.

# Grand Island Range (1917)

Grand Island is a large island that is located just a short distance upstream of Niagara Falls between New York and Canada. The Grand Island Range Lighthouse is located at the Buffalo Launch Club on Grand Island. Built in 1917 as a pair of range lights, the front range was a wooden light and a skeleton tower was constructed for the rear range light. The light is no longer in service, but can seen by taking Grand Island Boulevard to I-190, to the Buffalo Launch Club, located on Bush Road.

Grand Island Range – Grand Island Range Light is located just upstream from Niagara Falls, at the Buffalo Launch Club and was built in 1917.

# Dunkirk Pierhead (1939)

The Dunkirk Pierhead Light was built in 1939 and replaced the skeleton tower, which is on display at the grounds of the Dunkirk Lighthouse. The cylindrical D9 tower is white with a narrow red band. The beacon gives off a red flash every six seconds and has a focal plane height of 36 feet above sea level. The tower is managed by the U. S. Coast Guard and is adjacent to the Dunkirk Lighthouse.

Dunkirk Pier – Constructed in 1939, the short tower flashes red every six seconds and is located just north of the Dunkirk Light on Lake Erie.

# Nine - Lost Beacons of New York

An interesting and important piece of New York's maritime history is the fallen lighthouses. These lighthouses played too important a role to be forgotten. These lost beacons were constructed between 1827 and 1894, just after the Erie Canal was constructed. What follows are 15 vignettes on the fallen but not forgotten lighthouses. This chapter does not include those lighthouses that were rebuilt or replaced because of disrepair or faulty design and still remain an aid to navigation or historical landmark in New York.

## Throg's Neck (1827, 1906)

Figure 9-1. Throg's Neck.
*Courtesy U.S. Coast Guard.*

The area that marks the entrance to the East River is known as Throg's Neck. With the land forming a natural pier, construction of the lighthouse began in 1826. The original tower and keeper's house was torn down in 1835 to make room for Fort Schuyler. A temporary wooden tower was constructed. The lighting apparatus consisted of eleven lamps with spherical reflectors. In 1890, a skeleton tower was erected and outfitted with a Fifth-Order lens with a fixed white lamp. In 1906, a small brick tower with a Fourth-Order lens replaced the skeleton tower. The light was discontinued in 1934 and was replaced with a small skeleton tower with a small lamp. Today, a small skeleton tower stands where the original lighthouse once stood.

## Fort Thompkins (1828, 1873)

Figure 9-2. Fort Thompkins.
*Courtesy U.S. Coast Guard.*

The Fort Thompkins Lighthouse, established in 1828, is the second oldest beacon that was decommissioned and removed. This 40-foot lighthouse, located at the entrance to New York harbor at the Narrows, greeted mariners and immigrants arriving in America since it pre-dated the Statue of Liberty. Located on Staten Island, the Fort Thompkins beacon was initially equipped with twelve lamps and reflectors. It was updated in 1855 with a Fourth-Order lens. In 1863 during artillery practice at the fort, the lighthouse lantern glass was seriously damaged. By 1873, a new gingerbread dwelling was built and all the old structures were torn down. On April 28, 1898, the light was extinguished for four months as a safety measure during the Spanish-American War. The light and the fog signal continued to operate until the mid-1960s, when the construction of the Verrazano Narrows Bridge made the lighthouse obsolete.

## Stuyvesant (1829, 1836, 1868)

Figure 9-3. Stuyvesant.
*Courtesy U.S. Coast Guard.*

In March 1832, an ice jam on the Hudson River, upstream of the Stuyvesant Lighthouse, broke and sent a tsunami-like wave that destroyed everything in its path. Since there was no warning of the deluge, four members of the keeper's family drowned as they were swept downstream. A new four-room stone structure was completed in 1836, and the lighthouse was equipped with five lamps and thirteen three-quarter-inch reflectors. In 1854, it was upgraded with a Sixth-Order lens. The lighthouse was rebuilt for third time in 1868, but the Sixth-Order lens remained. In 1902 an ice jam formed between Coxsackie and Stuyvesant; when the ice broke, the lighthouse dwelling was swept away. Fortunately the keeper, Edwin McAllister, and his family were not at the lighthouse at the time of the ice break. The lighthouse was discontinued in 1933 and was replaced with a skeleton tower. It was torn down shortly thereafter.

## Coxsackie (1830)

Figure 9-4. Coxsackie.
*Courtesy U.S. Coast Guard.*

Completed in 1830 at a height of 38 feet above the river, Coxsackie was equipped with a fixed white light that was magnified with seven, fourteen-inch reflectors. Similar to Stuyvesant, the Coxsackie lighthouse was severely damaged from spring ice flows. During the winter of 1903, Keeper Jerome McDougall reported that blocks of ice and rushing water smashed the north wall of the lighthouse, creating a huge hole. This caused the first floor to fill with water and caused the west wall to collapse. Many stones in the foundation were also displaced, which caused one of the station's outhouses to be swept away in the Hudson. The second outhouse was crushed onsite. Repairs to the station were completed by June 1903. By 1940, the light was discontinued and replaced by a skeleton tower. Eventually the lighthouse was torn down.

## Four Mile Point (1831)

As directed by the Fifth Auditor, Stephen Pleasanton, two lighthouses were proposed; one at North Brother in the East River of New York City and one at Four Mile Point in the Hudson River. In 1838, the station was illuminated with seven lamps and parabolic reflectors. A new 25-foot iron structure was erected in 1880. An acetylene light was installed in 1918 and operated until 1928, when a skeleton tower was erected. In 1932, Donald Greene purchased the lighthouse for $1,100. Presently, only the keeper's dwelling remains.

## Bergen Point (1849, 1859)

Built on a 60-foot diameter caisson in 1849, the Bergen Point Lighthouse is located at the junction of Newark Bay and Kill Van Kull, just 50 feet from the New York and New Jersey border. The light station consisted of a two-story building and a wooden tower, which had an octagonal lantern room. When the house settled in the center, the cost to repair the damage was estimated at $20,000. Shortly after the assessment, the rebuilding effort began in 1857 and was completed in 1859. A large fog bell was added to replace a small hand struck bell in 1873. The station was discontinued in 1949 due to the widening of the Kill Van Kull. Bergen Point was replaced by a skeleton tower and eventually it was torn down.

## West Point (1853, 1872)

A 32-foot iron beacon was built in 1853 and equipped with a Sixth-Order lens with a fixed white light. The structure was erected at Gees Point on the west side of the Hudson River. The river bottom near the shore drops from 50 to 80 feet, which allows ships to navigate close to the point. In 1872, a 20-foot wooden hexagonal tower was erected and refitted with a Sixth-Order lens. In 1888, a machine-operated fog signal was added to the station. In July 1921, the ship, Phillip Mehrhof, smashed the fog signal, because it was too close to the water's edge. The West Point Lighthouse was discontinued in 1946 and was replaced by a skeleton tower.

## Gardiner's Island (1854)

Gardiner's Island Lighthouse was established to guide vessels through the north end of Gardiner's Bay in Long Island. Work on the brick lighthouse began early in 1854 and was completed by December. The keeper's quarters had a circular tower attached to the rear of the residence. The tower had to be accessed from outside. Because of erosion and the sea lapping at its foundation, the lighthouse was abandoned on March 8, 1894. Two months later, a gas-lighted buoy moored in 72 feet of water replaced the beacon.

## Horseshoe Reef (1856)

At one time, the Horseshoe Reef Lighthouse in Buffalo stood as an island in foreign waters. Thanks to Buffalo native President Millard Fillmore, an agreement was reached with the Queen of England and the border was changed. The remains of Horseshoe Reef are located at the junction of Lake Erie and the Niagara River. Because the growing activity of lake traffic, ships headed down the river with lumber and other goods to the docks at Black Rock, which was an expanding community in Buffalo. Shortly after Black Rock Channel was walled off from the Niagara River in 1920, the Horseshoe Reef was extinguished. In time, the wooden portions of the lighthouse decayed and disappeared and all that remains is the steel framework.

## Shinnecock Bay (1858)

Figure 9-5. Shinnecock Bay.
*Courtesy U.S. Coast Guard.*

One of great coastal lighthouses was erected in 1858 on Shinnecock Bay. Lt. J.C. Duane of the Corps of Engineers built the red brick tower, which rose 150 feet. The fixed white light was positioned 160 feet above mean high water. Located roughly midway between Fire Island and Montauk Point, Shinnecock Lighthouse had an important role in navigation and was equipped with a large First-Order lens. During the mid 1800s, it was the second tallest light in New York State. The fixed white light was changed to a flashing light in 1901 to help mariners distinguish between the lighthouse and other ships. In 1907, the light source was changed from oil to incandescent vapor, which raised its intensity from 12,100- to 45,600-candlepower.

Improvements in New York's main shipping channel made Shinnecock's beacon unnecessary. In 1931, the light was extinguished, replaced with a skeleton tower, and turned over to the U.S. Department of Agriculture. The tower was found unsafe and holes were drilled through the wall and a large section was removed from side near the base. Timbers that used to shore up the tower were soaked with gasoline and burned down. On December 23, 1948 the lighthouse leaned over and crashed to the ground.

# North Brother Island (1869)

Figure 9-6. North Brother Island.
*Courtesy U.S. Coast Guard.*

North Brother Island is located near the entrance to Hell's Gate along the East River. As a dangerous area for ships, many attempts to purchase the land to build a lighthouse were made. Edward Ackerman, the owner of the island, refused to sell the island on any terms. Offers to purchase the land lasted almost forty years but in 1868, the State of New York interceded and was successful in buying the parcel. The lighthouse complex consisted of keeper's quarters and an octagonal tower that rose fifty feet above sea level. The residence had four bedrooms, a kitchen, dining room, sitting room, pantry, and oil room. In 1889, a fog bell was added and in 1900, a Fourth-Order Fresnel lens was added.

Still, this area claimed countless numbers of vessels. On June 15, 1904, the *General Slocum* burned and rammed into North Brother Island. Doctors, nurses, and numerous employees of the local hospital staff helped save 155 lives; but over 1,000 perished aboard the General Slocum. In 1953 the lighthouse was discontinued and replaced with a white tower. The badly deteriorated dwelling stands on the southern side of the island.

# Buffalo Breakwater (1872)

Figure 9-7. Buffalo Breakwater.
*Courtesy U.S. Coast Guard.*

A detached 4000-foot breakwater was built in the Buffalo Harbor in 1868. In 1871, a 40-foot square crib was sunk at the end of the breakwater, which served as the foundation for Breakwater Lighthouse. After six courses of stone were added and allowed to settle, the new light was equipped with a Fourth-Order red beacon, located thirty-seven feet above Lake Erie. The Buffalo Life Saving Station set up quarters in 1879 on the lighthouse land and an upgrade to an incandescent oil lamp was made in 1855. In 1893, a steam signal replaced the fog bell.

The breakwater had taken a beating from the shipping traffic. It was hit by a tug in 1899; by a barge in 1900; by a freighter in 1909; and in 1910 by a steamer. The U.S. Army Corps of Engineers granted permission in 1914 to install Black Rock Ship Channel to control traffic around the old tower. On July 26, 1958 a huge lake freighter, the *Frontenac*, collided with the wall and tilted the lighthouse fifteen degrees. Although it was automated in 1960, it was deactivated in 1985.

# Hell's Gate (1884)

One of the first vessels to sink while entering the rock-infested waters of Hell's Gate was the British ship the H.M.S. *Hussar*. The 114-foot frigate was sailing toward Pot Rock and sank with $4 million worth of gold and silver. In 1855, construction began on a 255-foot iron tower. The tower contained nine electric lights, totaling 6,000 candlepower. But the tower was plagued with problems from the start. The light began to malfunction; one of the support towers lifted in place, and one of the cables separated. The light was discontinued in 1888 and it was replaced with a wooden tower.

# Danskammer Point (1885)

Located on the west side of the Hudson River, near Newburgh Bay, a 65-foot tall lighthouse was constructed at Danskammer Point. The name *Danskammer Point* is derived from the Dutch who, in the 1600s, observed this point of land was important to the Waoranecks who lived in the area. The Dutch recorded that these natives would gather at the point to dance before a hunt.

James Tole was appointed the first keeper, but after viewing his one-room quarters, he decided not to stay. His replacement was the assistant keeper, James West, who chose to live with his family in a nearby home. On July 11, 1914, Keeper West heard a roar and witnessed a blinding lightning flash. The bolt hit the tower, ran down one of the posts, shattered roof shingles, and struck West. He was thrown from his chair, paralyzing his left side. After the doctor examined him, he found a burn mark that reached from under his right arm and leg to his ankle. After repairs to the tower a lightning rod were made, West discovered that the lighthouse was struck in four places only a year later. Fortunately, West was away from his duty at the time of the second incident. The light was discontinued in 1925 and was replaced by a 53-foot tower. Today, there is power plant at Danskammer Point. It is also an excellent location for bird watching, as many Bald Eagles like to perch in this area.

# Rockland Lake (1894)

Located on the Hudson River near Rockland Lake Landing is a shallow oyster bed. Until 1880, steamboats were side-wheeled and navigated well in shallow water. But the newer steam vessels required more depth for navigation. Ship pilots and maritime interest groups petitioned the Lighthouse Board to erect a lighthouse at the eastern end of the shoal. Construction of the conical, cast-iron lighthouse began by driving 66 piles in a circular pattern into the river bottom. An iron caisson was floated, sank around the piles, and then was filled. Once the tower was completed, it was equipped with a Fourth-Order lens. Two years later a machine-operated fog bell was added. To secure the caisson, 200 tons of riprap stone were dumped to assist against erosion. From November to December 1894, another 1,200 tons of stone were placed on the north side to act as an icebreaker. At that time, inspectors noticed that the tower was leaning approximately nine inches in the northwesterly direction. The engineers speculated that the riprap caused the bottom to settle and caused the tower to lean. In 1906 an additional 3,000 tons were placed around the lighthouse. Despite many problems, the lighthouse continued to operate until 1923, when it was removed and replaced by a tower.

# Ten – Keeper's Life

Most of the men who manned the lighthouses in United States came from the sea. They were often sailors who had traveled around the world and after a lifetime at sea, dreamed of "swallowing an anchor" and finding a port to call home. From the first lighthouse in America, until Abraham Lincoln became President, all keepers were appointed by the President of the United States.

Did you ever wonder what it was like to be a lighthouse keeper 100 years ago? Can you imagine the life working on an isolated shore, such at Montauk Point or up along the Great Lakes?

Truly, lighthouse keeping is a solitary profession. Often the keepers did not see visitors for many weeks. The job demanded a great deal of routine, as documented in the keepers' logs. Keepers were devoted to their duties. They always stayed at the station, no matter what the situation or the weather presented. The life as a keeper was one of bravery, loyalty, and humble service.

In 1876, the Lighthouse Service began to distribute books to isolated stations through small, traveling lending libraries. Using supply boats, called tenders, they moved the libraries from station to station. The tenders were general purpose sailing vessels, named after different plants or flowers such as *Lilac, Iris, Geranium, Cactus* or *Juniper*. Eventually the government had specialized vessels to carry supplies, such as oil, coal, food and mail, to the keepers and their families. The tenders also set buoys and worked in search and rescue.

Although some stations were more isolated than others, it was important for keepers to educate their children. In some cases, a part-time tutor lived with a family for part of a year. In others, keepers were able to transfer to a lighthouse that was closer to a community with a school.

Some lighthouses were situated on islands that afforded the luxury of fertile soil for growing grass that allowed goats or cows to graze. In some cases the keepers hauled dirt from the mainland in barrels and boxes grew vegetables or flowers. At other locations, bird life provided the fertilizer to grow almost anything, such as turnips, radishes, onions, tomatoes and even potatoes.

Most sailors who became keepers had other skills such as fishing for salmon, sardines, and caviar. A good example was the Hill family who served at the Crossover Island Lighthouse. They caught, skinned, and dried up to 200 eels a day during the summer months.

During World War I, the Lighthouse Service encouraged keepers to grow gardens in because food supplies were scarce. The Lighthouse Service did not discourage keepers from engaging in outside work as long as the station was in good order and they were present to light the tower at sunset. Some keepers' wives collected shells, encased them in frames, and sold them to tourists. Before environmental regulations, eggs were collected and sold at local general stores or bartered for other goods.

Figure 10-1. Keeper's Dwelling

### Born in a Lighthouse – Robert Brunner

My father, Emil Brunner, had joined the U.S. Lighthouse Service in the early 1920s, before the Great Depression. He served as keeper at many stations in New York and New Jersey. When the Depression broke out, he was keeper at Stratford Shoals Light Station off the shore of Connecticut. Eventually, my father, mother, and three children were given the option to move to the Hudson-Athens Lighthouse, which was listed as a 'family station.' The station had eight rooms, four of which were bedrooms, and a full cellar. An oyster boat with all our belongings moved my family. I remember my mom recalling how my father had to row ashore to Athens to Dr. Cooper and Mrs. Baker to assist in my delivery.

The task of getting four children to school grew very difficult, especially in bad weather months. My parents decided to purchase a home on Third Avenue in Athens where we lived with our mother while our father lived at the lighthouse. Dad would come ashore if the weather permitted. We spent a lot of days during the summer at the lighthouse. My father would always keep us busy polishing brass or fishing. I remember my mother telling me many times the reason they had to move to shore was so they could afford to keep me in baby bottles because I would drop them out of my carriage onto the stone decking and they would break.

There was no electricity, so oil was standard equipment. The lamp in the tower was set on a revolving table and was magnified by prisms to increase it power. The revolving table was powered by a system of weights similar to a grandfather clock that had to be wound up every six hours. In 1946, they put in telephone and an electric line to the lighthouse from Athens. You could call ashore if you needed anything. The coal furnace was changed to oil and the oil lamp was put away."

Figure 10-2. Cover of *Saturday Evening Post*.

## A Family Affair

Lighthouse keeping was usually a family endeavor, where one or more members of the family knew how to operate the light, filling in when the keeper was away or during emergencies. Often lighthouses were tended by husband and wife teams. Wives were often called to fill for their husbands, and they proved they were highly capable of even the most strenuous duties.

One example was the Walker family, who transferred to the Robbins Reef station in 1855. Mrs. Kate Walker qualified as an assistant keeper while she and her husband served at Sandy Hook. She became the keeper of the Robbins Reef Light in Staten Island by substituting temporarily for husband who caught pneumonia and was hospitalized on the mainland. She faithfully tended the light and when her husband died, several keepers turned down the position because the station was too remote. The Lighthouse Serivice had no choice but to appoint her keeper. For about 30 years, she tended the light and raised two children. She estimated that during her tenure, she rescued 50 people from sudden storms and carelessness that ended up on the rocks around Robbins Reef. Mrs. Walker retired in 1919.

New York State records show that 19 women served as keepers for at least one year. Catherine Murdock had the longest tenure of any of the women by working 50 years at the Rondout Creek Lighthouse.

One problem and constant danger that keepers faced were from birds. The environment attracted from the very small songbirds to the larger herons or cranes. Most common were ducks and geese flying along the coastline in flocks. Lighthouses were not damaged very often by songbirds; but when ducks and larger shore birds flew into glass lens towers, they did considerable damage. There are several instances in lighthouse records of flying birds cracking prism lens. To mitigate any future damage, the Lighthouse Service ordered heavy wire screens to be installed on the exterior of lanterns.

## Patrolling Barnegat

Wild, wild the storm, and the sea high running,
Steady the roar of the gale, with incessant undertone muttering,
Shouts of demoniac laughter fitfully piercing and peeling,
Waves, air, midnight, their savagest trinity lashing,
Out in the shadows there milk-white combs careering,
On beachy slush and sand spirits of snow fierce slanting,
Where through the murk the easterly death-wind breasting,
Through cutting swirl and spray watchful and firm advancing,
(That in the distance! is red signal flaring?)
Slush and sand of the beach tireless till daylight wending,
Steady, slowly, through hoarse roar never remitting,
Along the midnight edge by those milk-white combs careering,
A group of dim, weird forms, struggling, the night confronting,
That savage trinity warily watching.

— Walt Whitman

Figure 10-3. Life Saving
Service Patrolling

## Keeper's Log

Lighthouse keepers were required after 1872 to post a daily log in a ledger, which was supplied by the Lighthouse Service. Previously, keeping the light involved mostly manual labor but now their tasks required them to read and write. Instructions for keeping the log were pasted on the inside front cover of the log.

Keepers interpreted the instructions in many different ways. Most recorded only the weather, while others included details about cleaning and repairing the station. Some identified every ship that passed by or supply boat that arrived, and some even included personal information like family illnesses, school achievements or church attendance. All keepers recorded disasters such ships going aground or seamen drowning.

Many logs contained pasted newspaper clippings, so reading a keeper's log was much like reading a history textbook. Personal letters were commonly found between pages. While some keepers wrote their names at the top or bottom of each entry, others never identified themselves at all. These logs were truly as individual as the keepers. All are interesting accounts of keepers' lives and their families and the local history surrounding their lighthouses.

# Eleven – Epilog

The peaceful view from the pinnacle of Turtle Hill in Montauk Point is a good place to embrace New York's premier maritime gems gracing our coastal and inland waterways. I hope that I have succeeded in helping you gain insight into the history of New York and our lighthouses. Hopefully you can appreciate the beauty of New York's coastal environs and lighthouses through these photographs and stories.

The call to be on or near the water, photographing and writing about lighthouses, is my passion. And I hope my enthusiasm is contagious. To fully experience the beauty and charm of these lighthouses, why not take a guided tour offered by a local preservation group? The Lighthouse Society of Long Island or the Hudson Valley Lighthouse groups are just two of many that maintain websites, where tours are posted. Why not bookmark the Appendix or Web Site Resource Section as you begin to travel and explore these New York lights? Experience the sights and sounds of a lighthouse keeper as you spend the night at Saugerties, Long Beach, Tibbetts Point or Selkirk. Explore one of the exquisite museums that host tours and contain lighthouse and nautical artifacts: Hudson River Maritime Museum, Seaway Trail Discovery Center, and Lake Champlain Maritime Museum. Discover the museum and gift shop at Montauk Point Lighthouse, a wonderful year-round destination.

After falling in love with a lighthouse, I hope you will help in preserving it for future generations. Consider joining a local lighthouse preservation society and begin to support them. Get involved with renovating, painting, or landscaping projects. Assist at one of their volunteer days or weekends. The benefits are multifold. It is only through the volunteers at the preservation societies that the New York lighthouses will remain for our children and our grandchildren. In addition to preserving the New York lights, there are many national lighthouse societies to support. These are listed in Appendix Two.

If you have especially enjoyed a photo found in this book, individual prints may be ordered on my website **www.RickTuers.com.**

# Appendices

Listed in the appendices are maps, guides, and handbooks for various New York lighthouses. There is also is a list of maritime museums and useful web links to assist with your visits to the many great lighthouses in New York and beyond. There are resources of national, regional and local preservation groups, should you wish to support them and volunteer. As always, another great source of supplemental material may be found on various Internet sites. Many lighthouses have their own home page, which contain information each lighthouse, including tours, hours of operation, and directions for travel.

## Appendix One-

## Maps, Guides, and Handbooks to Locate the Lights

1. *Lighthouses of the United States* – An illustrated map and directory to all standing lighthouses in the United States.
2. *America's Atlantic Coast Lighthouses* – Contains directions to lighthouses located in thirteen states along the Atlantic Ocean. Written by Kenneth Kochel.
3. *Staying at a Lighthouse, Americas Romantic and Historic Lighthouse Inns* – Great resource written by John Grant in conjunction with a PBS presentation.
4. *New York State Atlas and Gazetteer* – Contains topographic maps of the entire State of New York.
5. *Follow the Hudson River Lighthouse Trail* – Written by the Hudson River Lighthouse Coalition. Contains web links to find schedules for lighthouse tours. www.hudsonlights.com
6. *Maritime Museums of North America* – A great reference to finding information on America's maritime history. Written by Robert Smith.
7. *A Lighthouse Traveler's Guide to Eastern Great Lakes* – Photographs, maps and directions to 100 Canadian and American lighthouses on Lakes Erie and Ontario. This book is one of several done by Penrose family on the Great Lakes.
8. *A Listing of All Existing U.S. Lighthouses* – A great check list to use as you make your lighthouse visits. Written by Bob and Sandra Shaklin.
9. *New Jersey Lighthouse Guide* – Written by New Jersey and You, Perfect Together, an informative guide to the 20 New Jersey lighthouses. www.visitnj.org
10. *Lighthouses of New York* – Guide to the Greater New York Harbor, Hudson River, and Long Island. Written by a good friend, Jim Crowley.
11. *Lighthouses of New York* – A Guide to Thirty-three of the New York Lighthouses. Written by Bruce Roberts and Ray Jones.

# Appendix Two-

# Lighthouse Preservation Groups

## National & Regional Organizations

American Lighthouse Foundation
P.O. Box 889
Wells, MA 04090
207-646-0515
www.lighthousefoundation.org

Lighthouse Preservation Society
P.O. Box 736
Rockport, MA 01966
800-727-BEAM

Long Island Chapter, US Lighthouse Society
29745 Main Road
Cutchogue, NY 11935
631-207-4331
www.lilighthousesociety.org

National Lighthouse Center & Museum
One Lighthouse Plaza
Staten Island, NY 10301
718-556-1681
www.lighthousemuseum.org

National Maritime Historical Society
5 John Walsh Blvd.
Peekskill, NY 10560
800-221-6647
www.seahistory.org

United States Lighthouse Society
244 Kearney Street
San Francisco, CA 94108
415-362-7255
www.uslhs.org

## Local Groups

Buffalo Lighthouse Association
One Fuhrmann Blvd
Buffalo, NY 14203
716-947-9126
www.buffalohistoryworks.com/light

Cedar Island Preservation Committee
P.O. Box 440
East Hampton, NY 11937
631-645-5230

Charlotte-Genesee Lighthouse Museum
70 Lighthouse Street
Rochester, NY 14612
716-621-6179
http://www.geneseelighthouse.org/

Dunkirk Lighthouse & Veterans Park
P.O. Box 69 – One Lighthouse Point Drive
Dunkirk, NY 14048
716-366-5050
www.dunkirklighthouse.com

Fire Island Lighthouse Preservation Society
4640 Captree Island
Captree Island, NY 11702-4601
631-661-4876
www.fireislandlighthouse.com

Friends of Thirty Mile Point Lighthouse
P.O. Box 20
Barker, NY 14012
716-795-3885

Horton Point Lighthouse & Museum
Southold Historical Society
P.O. Box 1
Southold, NY 11971
631-765-5500
www.southoldparkdistrict.com

Hudson-Athens Lighthouse Preservation Society
Two First Street
Athens, NY 12015
518-828-5294
www.hudsonathenslighthouse.org

Huntington Lighthouse Preservation Society
P.O. Box 2454
Halesite, NY 11743
631-421-1985
www.huntingtonlighthouse.org

Long Beach Lighthouse
c/o East End Seaport Museum
P.O. Box 624
Greenport, NY 11944
631-477-2100
www.eastendseaport.org

Montauk Point Lighthouse
Montauk Historical Society
P.O. 943
Montauk, NY 11954
www.montauklighthouse.com

Old Fort Niagara
P.O. Box 169
Youngstown, NY 14714
716-745-7611

Rondout Lighthouse
c/o Hudson River Maritime Museum
50 Rondout Landing
Kingston, NY 12401
845-338-0071
www.hrmm.org

Saugerties Lighthouse Conservancy
P.O. Box 654
Saugerties, NY 12477
845-246-4380
www.saugertieslighthouse.com

Save the Esopus Lighthouse Commission
P.O. Box 1290
Port Ewan, NY 12466
845-338-2435
www.esopusmeadowslighthouse.org

Selkirk Lighthouse
P.O. Box 228
Pulaski, NY 13142
315-298-6688

Sodus Bay Lighthouse Museum
7606 N. Ontario Street
Sodus Point, NY 14555
315-483-4936
www.maine.com/lights/sodus.htm

Tarrytown Lighthouse Museum
Kingsland Point Park
Route 9
Sleepy Hollow, NY 10591
914-366-5109
www.hudsonlights.com/tarrytown.htm

Tibbetts Pt. Historical Society
P.O. Box 683
Cape Vincent, NY 13618
315-654-2700

---

# Appendix Three –

# Maritime Museums

American Merchant Marine Museum
U.S. Merchant Marine Academy
Kings Point, NY 11024
516-773-5515
www.usmma.edu/museum

Cold Spring Harbor Whaling Museum
Main Street, P. O. Box 25
Cold Spring Harbor, NY 11724
631-367-3418
www.cshwhalingmuseum.org

D & H Canal Historical Society
P.O. Box 23
High Falls, NY 12440
845-687-9311
www.canalmuseum.org

Erie Canal Discovery Center
24 Church Street
Lockport, NY 14094
716-434-7433
www.eriecanaldiscoverycenter.org

H. Lee White Marine Museum
P.O. Box 101
Oswego, NY 13126
315-342-0480
www.hleewhitemarinemuseum.com

Lake Champlain Maritime Museum
4472 Basin Harbor Road
Vergennes, VT 05491
802-475-2022
www.lcmm.org

Long Island Maritime Museum
P.O. Box 184, 86 West Avenue
West Sayville, NY 11796
631-HISTORY
www.limaritime.org

Long Island Seaport & Eco. Center
P.O. Box 750
Port Jefferson, NY 11777
631-474-4725
www.lisec.org

Lower Lakes Marine Historical Society
66 Erie Street
Buffalo, NY 14202
716-849-0914
www.llmhs.org

Seaway Trail and Discovery Center
P.O. Box 660
Sacketts Harbor, NY 13685
315-646-1000
www.seawaytrail.com

South Street Seaport
12 Fulton Street
New York, NY 10038
212-748-8600
www.southstseaport.org

Waterfront Center
One West End Avenue
Oyster Bay, NY 11771
516-922-7245
www.thewaterfrontcenter.org

---

# Appendix Four –

## Lighthouse and Maritime Links

| | |
|---|---|
| U.S. Coast Guard: | www.uscg.mil/history/h_lhindex.html |
| U.S. Life Saving Service: | www.uslife-savingservice.org |
| Light Ships: | www.uscg.mil/history/Lightship_Index.html |
| National Maritime History: | www.seahistory.org |
| Hudson River: | www.hudsonlights.com |
| Hudson River Maritime: | www.hrmm.org |
| Long Island: | www.longislandlighthouses.com |
| Long Island Viewing Guide: | www.scroope.net/lighthouses/longisland.htm |
| Montauk Point: | www.montaukpoint.com |
| California: | www.erealms.com/california-lighthouses/index.html |
| Chesapeake Bay: | www.cheslights.org |
| Florida: | www.floridalighthouses.org |
| Great Lakes: | www.gllka.com |
| New Jersey: | www.njlighthouses.net |
| Maine: | www.lighthouse.cc/me.html |
| Outer Banks: | www.outer-banks.com/lighthouse-society |
| Australia: | www.lighthouse.net.au/lights/index.htm |
| New Brunswick: | www.nblighthouses.com |
| World Lighthouse Society: | www.worldlighthouses.org |
| World Lighthouses: | www.vl-lighthouses.org |

# Bibliography

Adamson, Hans Christian. *Keepers of the Lights – The Saga of Our Lighthouses, Lightships, and the Men Who Guide Those Who Sail the Sea.* New York: Greenberg, 1955.

Bachand, Robert G. *Northeast Lights, Lighthouses and Lightships (Rhode Island to Cape May).* Norwalk, Connecticut: Sea Sports Publications, 1989.

Bathhurst, Bella. *The Lighthouse Stevensons.* New York: Harper Collins Publishers, 1999.

Beaver, Patrick. *A History of Lighthouses.* Secaucus, New Jersey: Citadel Press, 1971.

Berger, Todd R. *Lighthouses of the Great Lakes – Your Guide to the Region's Historic Lighthouses.* Stillwater, Minnesota: Voyageur Press, 2002.

Bond, L.E. *Statue of Liberty – Beacon of Promise.* Santa Barbara, California: Albion Publishing Group, 1990, 1992.

Clifford, George E. *Lake Champlain Lighthouses.* Plattsburgh, New York: Clinton County Historical Association, 1999.

Clifford, Mary Louise and J. Candace. *Women Who Kept the Lights – An Illustrated History of Female Lighthouse Keepers.* Williamsburg, Virginia: Cypress Communications, 1993.

Crompton, Samuel Willard and Michael J. Rhein, *The Ultimate Book of Lighthouses.* San Diego, California: Thunder Bay Press, 2003.

Crowley, Jim. *Lighthouses of New York.* Saugerties, New York: Hope Farm Press, 2000.

Gonzalez, Ellice B. *Storms, Ships & Surfmen, The Lifesavers of Fire Island.* Fort Washington, Pennsylvania: Eastern National, 2000.

Glunt, Ruth R. *Lighthouses and Legends of the Hudson.* Monroe, New York: Library Research Associates, Inc., 1990.

Hamilton, Harlan. *Lights & Legends – A Historical Guide to Lighthouses of Long Island Sound, Fishers Island Sound and Block Island Sound.* Stamford, Connecticut: Westcott Cove Publishing Co., 1987.

Harrison, Tim and Ray Jones. Lost *Lighthouses.* Guilford, Connecticut: Globe Pequot Press, 2000.

Holland, Francis Ross Jr. *America's Lighthouses – An Illustrated History.* New York: Dover Publications, 1972.

Hudson River Valley Commission of New York. *The Hudson River Lighthouses.* Albany, New York, 1967.

Kochel, Kenneth G. *America's Atlantic Coast Lighthouses.* Clearwater, Florida: Betken Publications, 1994.

Morganstein, Martin and J.H. Cregg. *Images of America – Erie Canal.* Charleston, South Carolina: Arcadia Publishing, 2001.

Merryman, J.H. *The United States Life-Saving Service-1880.* Silverthorne, Colorado: Vista Books, 1997.

Müller, Robert G. *Long Island's Lighthouses Past and Present.* Interluken, New York: Heart of the Lakes Publishing, 2004.

Nordhoff, Charles. *The Light-Houses of the United States in 1874.* Golden, Colorado: Outbooks, 1981.

Oleszewski, Wes. *Great Lakes Lighthouses American & Canadian.* Gwinn, Michican: Avery Color Studies, 1998.

Penrose, Laurie. *A Traveler's Guide to 100 Eastern Great Lakes Lighthouses.* Davidson, Michigan: Friede Publications, 1994.

Rattray, Jeannette E. *The Perils of the Port of New York.* New York: Dodd, Mead & Company, 1973.

Roberts, Bruce and Ray Jones. *Lighthouses of New York.* Guilford, Connecticut: Globe Pequot Press, 2006.

Roberts, Bruce and Ray Jones. *American Lighthouses – A Definitive Guide.* Guilford, Connecticut: The Globe Pequot Press, 1998.

Shanks, Ralph, Wick York, and Lisa Woo Shanks. *The U.S. Life-Saving Service.* Petaluma, California: Shanks & York, 1997.

Smith, Robert. *Maritime Museums of North America.* Annapolis, Maryland: Naval Institute Press, 1990.

Stanne, Stephen P., Roger G. Panette, Brian E. Forist. *The Hudson – An Illustrated Guide to the Living River.* New Brunswick, New Jersey: Rutgers University Press, 1996.

Swift, Hildegarde H., Lynd Ward. *The Little Red Lighthouse and the Great Gray Bridge.* New York: Voyager Books, 1970.

Tinney, James, Mary Burdette-Watkins. *Seaway Trail Lighthouses: An Illustrated Guide.* Sacketts Harbor, New York: Seaway Trail, Inc., 1989.

U.S. Department of Transportation. *U.S. Coast Guard, Light List – Volume 1 – Atlantic Coast.* Washington, D.C.: U.S. Government Printing Office, 1997.

Van Zandt, Roland. *Chronicles of the Hudson – Three Centuries of Travel and Adventure.* Hensonville, New York: Black Dome Press Corp., 1992.

# Lighthouse Glossary

**Aid to navigation** – Any device external to a vessel or aircraft specifically intended to assist navigators in determining their position or safe course or to warn them of danger or obstructions to navigation.

**Appropriation** – An act by the U.S. Congress authorizing money paid from the Treasury for purposes of a specific task, project, or study. A lighthouse project usually required several appropriations before construction could begin.

**Argand lamp** – Clean-burning oil lamp that was widely used in Lighthouse Service during the late eighteenth and early nineteenth century. The lamp was designed by French inventor Aimé Argand.

**Assistant keeper** – At the larger lighthouses, especially coastal lights, one or more assistant keepers were required to maintain the light station complex, keep lamps lit, and fog signals operating properly.

**Candle power** – A measure of the lighting intensity of lamps or lighting apparatus used in the lighthouse.

**Characteristic** – The identifying feature of a lighthouse beacon. To help mariners distinguish between different beacons, every location had distinct color or flashing sequence.

**Clamshell or bi-valve lenses** – Most Fresnel lenses are round, but some are flattened, resembling a clamshell or bi-valve.

**Clockworks mechanism** – A mechanical device that is similar to grandfather clock and is used to rotate a beacon or ring a fog bell. The mechanism needed to be manually set every four to six hours to maintain their use.

**Coast Guard** – Since 1939, the lighthouses and other aids to navigation in America have been the responsibility of the U.S. Coast Guard. Prior to the Coast Guard, all aids to navigation were operated by the Lighthouse Service.

**Decommissioned light** – A lighthouse which no longer functions as an aid-to-navigation and sometimes referred to as an extinguished light.

**Diaphone** – A powerful foghorn invented in Canada which produces a loud blast to warn mariners during periods of low visibility. The foghorn is operated by compressed air generated by steam, gas or oil engine.

**Establish** – The date that the light station was completed and the first lighting of the lamp.

**Fixed light** – A lighthouse beacon that shines constantly during its regular hours of operation is called a fixed light.

**Flashing light** – A lighthouse beacon that shows an on and off characteristic at a regular interval.

**Focal plane** – The height of the lighthouse lens focal point above sea-level.

**Fog bell** – A distinct sound signal, usually a horn, trumpet, or siren, used to warn vessels away from prominent headlands or navigational obstructions during fog or periods of low visibility.

**Fresnel lenses** – Invented in 1822 by Augustin Fresnel, a French physicist, which consists of a series of glass prisms supported by brass framework. The light reflected through the lenses will concentrate the light beam that can be viewed for distances up to 25 miles.

**Keeper** – A person who was responsible for all the operations at the light station. Lighthouse Keepers were appointed by the President of the United States or the Secretary of the Treasury prior to the Civil War.

**Lamp** – The lighting apparatus inside the lens. (Oil, kerosene vapor, or electric lamp).

**LAMP Program** – Lighthouse Automation Modernization Program was initiated in 1968 and was extended until 1989 to accelerate and standardize the remaining lighthouses for automation.

**Life Saving Service** – Service was established in 1876 by Miles Kimball and manned stations were set up primarily on ocean waters to rescue boaters from the ocean surf.

**Lighthouse** – An enclosed tower or building, constructed by the government, and designed to function as an aid-to-navigation.

**Lighthouse Board** – The Lighthouse Board, created in 1851, was a group of engineers, scientists, and military personnel who worked to modernize the Lighthouse Service's practices.

**Lighthouse Establishment** – Promoted by President George Washington, Congress passed legislation on August 7, 1789 which created the Lighthouse Establishment.

**Lighthouse Service** – A common term applied to different organizations that built or maintained the U.S. lighthouses from 1789 until 1939, when the Coast Guard was placed in charge.

**Light List** – An official Coast Guard list of aids to navigation along the coasts and inland waterways, featuring brief descriptions of the aid and precise locations.

**Lightships** – Equipped with their own beacons, usually displayed from a tall central mast, lightships were floating lighthouses. They marked shoals where construction of a lighthouse was impossible or prohibitively expensive.

**Light station** – A navigation facility with a light beacon, commonly referred to as a light or light station. Often interchanged with the lighthouse, but a light station might not include a keeper's quarter or fog signal.

**LORAN** – Short for Long-Range Aid to Navigation. LORAN is an electronic aid-to-navigation consisting of shore based radio transmitter. The LORAN communication system enables users to determine their position quickly and accurately day or night.

**Occulting or eclipsing light** – There are several ways to produce a beacon that appears to flash. One way is to occult or block the light at regular intervals, often with a rotating opaque panel.

**Range Lights** – A pair of lighthouses which indicate a safe course when lined up one above the other. Sometimes one or both may be a simple skeleton tower.

**Rip rap** – Large stones that are placed around the lighthouse or the foundation to reduce the wave energy and protect against ice damage.

**SHORAN** – Abbreviation for Short Range Aid to Navigation and an electronic aid used similar to LORAN.

**Skeleton tower** – Iron or steel skeleton light towers consisting of four or more heavily braced metal legs topped with a lantern.

# Index